AGAINST *the* GRADE

Working on the Settle - Carlisle Railway

BOB SWALLOW

GREAT NORTHERN

Great Northern Books
PO Box 213, Ilkley, LS29 9WS
www.greatnorthernbooks.co.uk

ISBN: 978 1 905080 89 2

Design and layout: David Burrill

CIP Data
A catalogue for this book is available from
the British Library

*For an application form to join FoSCL
(The Friends of the Settle-Carlisle Line)
please send an sae to:
FoSCL Membership Secretary,
5 Dewhirst Road, Brighouse,
W. Yorks HD6 4BA
or see the website www.foscl.co.uk*

Contents

Photos on preliminary pages:
Pages 2/3: Limestone pavement and Ribblehead viaduct.
Page 4: Against the grade – 5029 'Nunney Castle' struggles mightily
above Stainforth, Ribblesdale, in 1994.

Foreword
by Mike Harding

I came to live at Railway Cottages, Selside in the August of 1971 and, apart from moving up-line to Dent for a number of years, I have lived in the Dales and close by the Settle-Carlisle ever since.

From the very first I was afflicted by Settle-Carlisleitis. I became fascinated by the line and its stories and am glad to say that my two young grandsons at the ripe old ages of five and six are similarly besotted. It is the kind of line that does that to you. Its official history is grand and stirring enough: the Midland Railway General Manager James Allport (later Sir James) and his Chief Civil Engineer John Crossley who together walked the proposed course of the line surveying it; the Welsh masons who came to dress the stone for the viaducts, leats and tunnels; the 6,000 nameless men and women who came to build the line by hand and whose bones lie mouldering alongside the permanent way; and the long fight to keep the line open in the face of bureaucratic ignorance have all been well documented.

But it is the human stories that have always set the Settle-Carlisle line apart from other lesser lines, and those you will find here in plenty; true gems told simply by men and women who have worked on the line or lived alongside it. This book is not just an invaluable piece of social history and railway folklore, it is a treasure trove of tales and a joy to read.

Introduction

Uncle Joe was an engine driver. It was easy to tell this from his eyes screwed up as they were from peering out the side of the cab. He had been in the top link from Blackpool Central to London Euston until his eyes began to fail. This would be around the time of World War 2. He used to say that his engine was the Midland Compound Number 1000, now in the National Collection at NRM York. I suspect what he meant was that he regularly drove it.

When I as a young lad knew him just prior to his retirement, he had been relegated to the Blackpool North/Fleetwood push and pull due to eyesight problems. This did have its advantages as several times I was smuggled on board the 0-4-4 tank fulfilling this duty to ride the ten miles or so to what was then a massive fishing port. I do remember enquiring of Uncle Joe as to the purpose of another tank engine of possibly 4-4-4 configuration which stood against the buffer stops at Blackpool North in a remote unused platform, its driving wheels now missing, a huge extension to the chimney disappearing through a hole cut in the glass roof. He thought for a few moments before advising that it was called 'Robert the Devil' and ventured out onto the mainline only at night-time.

"How," I enquired, "does it get under the bridges with that huge chimney?"

Silence for a moment or two then, "Well, it has a rubber coupling at the base of the chimney which allows it to be lowered to get underneath them."

This clearly satisfied my curiosity as I had it seems no more questions. Imagine Uncle Joe telling his mates about it next day. The engine was by the way a stationary boiler used for heating carriages coupled to it prior to them going into service on a cold winter's morning.

I was never employed on the railway though many members of my family were. I have a gold pocket watch still going, presented to my great-great-granddad by his staff on his retirement from the joint service of the Lancashire & Yorkshire and London & North Western Railways and dated February 9th 1895.

Granddad from the other side of the family was the goods superintendent for the LMS in Leeds, when he retired receiving a huge skeleton clock some three feet tall in the likeness of the frontage of Westminster Abbey, one side containing the chiming train, the other the going train. It was designed to stand on the massive mantle shelves so popular in large houses in the 1930s.

There is a tale about this clock, which was enclosed in a substantial glass dome that had to be removed to wind up the clock. This was easier said than done, a feat accomplished by licking ones fingers prior to pressing tight to the sides of the dome before lifting gingerly skyward.

Needless to say the dome got broken on at least one occasion so Granddad ordered another from Pilkingtons, the St Helen's glassmakers. Not trusting this to the tender mercies of a carrier, much less the railway, he took himself plus my then two young aunts to collect same. Returning to the station he deposited the dome carefully wrapped into a corner seat of the Leeds train, a

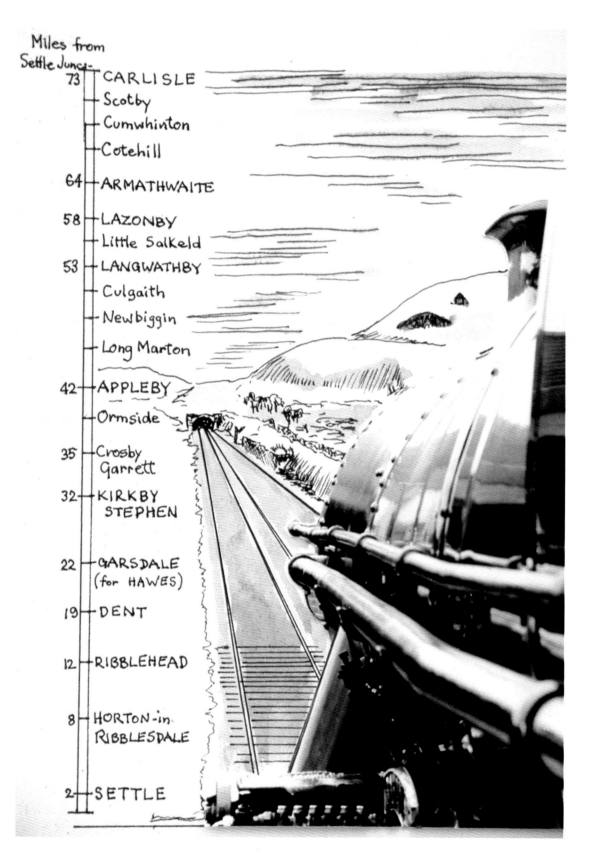

Miles from
Settle Junc.

73 — CARLISLE
— Scotby
— Cumwhinton
— Cotehill
64 — ARMATHWAITE
58 — LAZONBY
— Little Salkeld
53 — LANGWATHBY
— Culgaith
— Newbiggin
— Long Marton
42 — APPLEBY
— Ormside
35 — Crosby Garrett
32 — KIRKBY STEPHEN
22 — GARSDALE (for HAWES)
19 — DENT
12 — RIBBLEHEAD
8 — HORTON-in-RIBBLESDALE
2 — SETTLE

non-corridor variety, before departing for the gents on the platform. The guard blew his whistle, granddad returning in haste to land in the corner seat. He was a pillar of the church, my aunts never before having heard him swear. He made up for it that day.

So the seed was sown. For near thirty years I have been collecting railway anecdotes about the Settle-Carlisle Railway, initially for use in an audio-visual production promoting the line when it was under threat of closure. A second one followed in 1995 recounting many more of these stories, later dealing with the massive works undertaken to revitalise the railway.

During this time I have met a great many railwaymen and women, some retired, others still in the employ of Network, or Northern Rail. Without exception I have found them to be delighted to recount their tales, some of which date back to the 1940/50s and beyond. It is to them along with my long-time friend Dr W. R. (Bill) Mitchell MBE that this book is dedicated. It is doubtful if anyone else has written more about this line that refused to die.

My thanks are due to Mike Harding for writing the Foreword, Bill Mitchell for his help with the manuscript and retelling some of his tales, Peter Fox for his illustrations and photographs of some of the situations described, my wife Pauline for tolerating long absences in the study, and son-in-law Richard Wallbank for help with computer problems. An acknowledgement follows of all those who have allowed their stories – whether sad, nostalgic or so often hilarious – to be recounted. Please forgive me if I have through oversight omitted anyone.

By the way, lest you are not so far addicted, there is a highly contagious disease which strikes without warning those who become devotees of this railway. Settle-Carlisleitis is an affliction with no known cure. The condition may however be alleviated by frequent visits to the railway, reading the many learned tomes written upon it or simply by riding it in all weathers. And no, I am not on booking commission from Northern Rail.

Finally, many of the stories go back several decades, possibly playing tricks with the memory. Bill once told me never to forget the first rule of journalism. Never to let the facts get in the way of a good story. So that is my excuse if any reader thinks things happened otherwise!

Acknowledgements

Peter Ainsworth; Donald Alker; Dickie Birtle; Geoff Bounds; Alan Dugdale; Tony Eaton; Nancy Edmondson; Tony Freschini; Stanley Hall MBE; Ken Harper; George Hinchcliffe; Gordon Hodgson; the late George Horner; Ian Ibbotson; Paul Jameson; the late Alan King; Brenda Newby; John Reid; Gary Richards; Jimmy Richardson; Malcolm Sissons; Derek Soames; Mickey Venn; and David Ward.

Chapter One

Fun on the Platform

Dent, the highest main line station in England, can be a pig to get to, four and a bit miles from the village it purports to serve and six hundred feet above it, approached by a hairpin one in four road. An off-comer reputedly enquired of a local farmer why it had been so inconveniently sited. That worthy scratched his head doubtless seeking inspiration. Suddenly it dawned: "'appen they wanted it near the tracks."

Despite its location Dent could be a busy job for the porter with just the stationmaster to help. One such porter remembered from his time there dealing with a corpse. "I booked him single."

A porter's life

Derek Soames spent over fifty years working on the railway, initially as a porter. He left school at the age of thirteen to deliver groceries for the Co-op in Settle. It was a dead end job, so, passing Settle station one day, on impulse he spoke to John Banks the stationmaster to see if there was any chance of railway work. This was early June 1945. He filled in an application form, shortly after receiving a message to attend a medical at Glasgow, somewhere on another planet to a lad by now of fourteen. This would have meant cycling into Hellifield in the dark to catch the 3am Glasgow train, returning later at some unearthly hour. John Banks had already contacted the powers that be, and as a result Derek had his medical in Carlisle.

He started as a junior porter at Settle on 11 June 1945. In those days it was a busy station. Stationmaster; stationmaster's clerk; two porters; booking clerk; goods porter; goods clerk plus a wagon driver. Anything that arrived by passenger train was delivered by the porters on barrows. Larger items arriving by freight train were transported around town by the wagon.

There was animal feed for two 'provy' feed firms, Thornbers and Settle Farmers. Around five coal merchants worked out of the yard. Coal also arrived for the cotton mill at Langcliffe and for the gas works. John Moores, gents outfitters in the town, had several parcels each day. As junior porter this latter was very much Derek's province.

Pay day

Friday was pay day. The stationmaster at Settle was responsible for the wages of staff from Hellifield – around seventy folk – to Garsdale. After he had visited the bank, Martins in those days, to notify his requirements, the porter and his junior would make their way there with a two wheeled box barrow. Here they waited as a member of bank staff brought out a series of cash boxes which were then pushed back through the streets to the station. Imagine this now!

The stationmaster made up the cash for each location which was placed in an individual locked box before being transferred to the guard on a convenient train to transport north or south. He of course had to sign for this as did the receiving stationmaster.

Dawsons at Langcliffe Hall had several horses which over-wintered in the south before travelling by horseboxes up north in the spring. Geoffrey Dawson was editor of the Times newspaper so his main home was in London. The station staff received prior notice when these horseboxes were to travel north attached to a certain train. When the horses had been detrained at the cattle dock a groom would walk them to Langcliffe.

A roving commission

Derek continues the story:

"After a while it was decided that I should be more useful in a roving capacity. I had a spell at Gargrave, a busy spot. Several junior porters were called up for National Service, after which I moved to Hellifield as a junior relief porter. This gave me an area from Kildwick in the south to Garsdale in the north plus Morecambe and Heysham down the branch. Bolton Abbey was also on my patch.

A message would come through, 'Tomorrow you are at Garsdale.' No advice as to how to get there. You worked that out yourself. I've gone on engines and brake vans. I've gone many a mile on a push bike.

Why would they want another porter at Garsdale? Well of course in those days there were considerable numbers of people changing trains to the Wensleydale branch, some going through to Northallerton. It was our job to help them particularly when alighting from northbound trains to transfer to the island platform. There was never a bridge from one platform to the other so you had to be on your guard when taking passengers across the running lines. There was only one shop at Garsdale which still had lots of parcels arriving at the station requiring delivery."

The Garsdale joker

"There was always one long-serving member of staff pulling my leg. One tale I recall was being advised to walk down the Hawes branch during my lunch break as grouse were forever flying into the telephone wires running parallel to the rails and being killed. I might collect a brace to take

North end of Hellifield station – the logical starting point of the Settle-Carlisle railway from the south.

home. I walked a heck of a long way down the branch one lunchtime and found nothing. Frustrated, I decided to take a short cut across the fell. There were plenty of grouse to be seen then as I was between the beaters and the guns. I was not popular!"

Quarry work

"Another station at which I saw service was Horton in Ribblesdale, though most of my work was done at Helwith Bridge some two miles south. Here there were three quarries all rail connected. On the other hand none of them had any road access, just a track for the workers to get to the quarries. I found my way there by unofficially walking the lineside. I had to take the numbers of any wagons shunted there. Later I would record details of full ones leaving and their destinations.

There was a signal box controlling the triangular layout into the quarries, one of my jobs being to get water for the signalman in a two gallon galvanised can which I took up to the quarry to where a stream came out of a rockface. (This was before Health and Safety reared its head.) There was no purification plant, I simply took the can back to the box, a fair old trek.

Limestone was brought down from the quarry top at Foredale by self-acting incline to the kilns which strangely used coke rather than coal for the process. The finished product then travelled to Scotland to be used in steelmaking. Another quarry sent road chippings by rail to Stainforth Sidings where they were collected by a fleet of lorries. The rail journey they made must have been one of the shortest in the country, around two-and-a-half miles."

Tea break

Hellifield is the logical starting point of the Settle-Carlisle railway from the south. The Midland Railway who built their line to Scotland over the high Pennines was here joined by the Lancashire & Yorkshire coming up from Manchester via Blackburn. Hellifield grew dramatically with the coming of the railways, boasting two goods yards and at one stage two engine sheds, one belonging to each company.

At the time of our next tale back in 1948 it was still a large busy junction station, the stationmaster having under his care a staff of around seventy. Derek Soames was a junior porter at this time, having started his railway career during 1945 at Settle.

There was a tearoom on the long island platform, many trains stopping here just long enough for passengers to catch a porter's eye for a cup of tea. Now this was a good thing for a young porter, he being able as a member of staff to purchase such beverage for 1d whereas a member of the public was charged 1½ d. So Derek duly scampered off on behalf of an elderly lady, returning with a cup of tea just as the train was pulling out. Why is it that women never seem to have their money to hand? So he didn't get paid.

A couple of weeks passed until one day the stationmaster called him into his office.

"Now then young Soames, did you buy a cup of tea for a lady on a train and not get paid?"

Derek Soames and the cup of tea saga.

Derek thought quickly knowing he should not really have done this, so giving an evasive answer. "Well perhaps I did."

"Well," retorted the stationmaster, "this lady has written to me saying that a tall good looking young porter had obtained a cup of tea for her and she had not paid him, so she has enclosed a cheque for 2s 6d." Taking a cup of tea at today's prices as £1 – very cheap – this equates to around £30 for what Derek had paid. Nice work if you can get it!

A horticultural hobby

Some six miles further north is Settle station, famed for the long-serving stationmaster there, Jim Taylor. He had previously served in the same capacity at Horton in Ribblesdale, the next station north and some 340 feet higher than Settle, itself at 510 feet above sea level. Jim came from a family of market gardeners and took it upon himself to set out to win the best-kept station garden competition. To this end at Settle he hacked up part of the down platform to create larger flower beds. In his own words, "We didn't bother telling the management about this, just got on with it and presented them with a fait accompli." So successful was this ploy that first Horton then Settle won the best-kept station garden competition a total of sixteen times, plus for good measure, for best-kept station on several occasions.

It might not happen today, but in September 1951 stationmaster Jim Taylor and his wife provided gallons of coffee to fifty passengers stranded at Horton in Ribblesdale following a derailment. They duly received a letter of appreciation from head office.

Jim Taylor later moved to Settle station, which he made famous for its best-kept gardens. He even hacked up part of the down platform to create larger flower beds!

Jim Taylor receiving the best-kept station garden award – yet again! He won it no less than sixteen times for the gardens at Horton-in-Ribblesdale and Settle.

Improving the service

When Jim took over at Settle the express trains did not stop, although they did so at Appleby – the county town of Westmorland. This was a legacy of trains stopping at all county towns. As he pointed out, little Oakham – the county town of Rutland – had a far better service than Settle. He got nowhere with management for upwards of eighteen months in his efforts to have express trains stop at his station.

Eventually he got them convinced, one suspects through the well documented nuisance policy, where seniors give way to juniors just to get some peace and quiet. However when more trains did stop his bosses were amazed at the increased traffic he had generated.

Generating respect

The stationmaster of old was remembered as a much respected figure in the community. Very much the figurehead, Benny Ash at Settle at an earlier time was one such. Once a week he would arrange to collect the wages for station staff at several locations from a local bank. That apart he would stride up and down the platform when a train was in, letting everyone know he was boss. As soon as he had seen it safely on its way he would nip to the Golden Lion for a whisky.

We don't have stationmasters as such now but can you imagine them following the above criteria these days?

Inspections

Appleby along with Settle was classed as a large station. Norman Greenhow was traffic manager at the former when the area manager was due to make his annual inspection. There was one member of staff described to me as 'Not the brightest knife in the drawer.' Fred Marshall, relief signalman, suggested to Norman that he had better "hide him or they'll sack him and thee for employing him".

Again at Appleby, Harold there knew more about railways than most people can remember. Although not a member of staff he spent hours every day helping them. He had his own room (officially the mess room) known as Harold's Room where the kettle bubbled perpetually away and cars, railway vehicles and the like might be washed for a modest fee. Again the area manager's inspection was imminent so Harold was instructed to make himself scarce for a couple of hours. The area manager arrives, his first question, "Where's Harold?"

A slave to the weed

Billy Bannister lived at Stone House in the hamlet of Arten Gill two and a half miles from Dent station and several hundred feet below. He had started as a porter in Leeds before moving to

Dent. He soon qualified as a signalman and worked in Dent box for over thirty years. Each morning for thirty-five years he would roll nine cigarettes before going on duty. One for the start of his eight-hour shift, plus one for every hour thereafter. He was noted for being meticulous, a stickler for detail.

In all that time he never missed a shift and was only late twice. The first occasion was when his house caught fire, the second when he fell over the stile approaching Arten Gill viaduct and fractured his ankle, not too badly it seems, as he still hobbled to work.

A wild posting

Cecil Sanderson (Sandy) was the stationmaster at Dent from 2 June 1938 until 1945. This came about after having been called to Derby to meet Mr Hibbert, the operating superintendent, who remembered him as a Signalman Class 5 at Heysham Harbour. There were two vacancies for stationmaster, the other being Grange over Sands. He fancied the latter but was offered the former, which he knew from stints as a relief signalman at Selside and Dent Head. His new chief pointed out that this was a first posting for possibly six months. World War 2 put an end to promotion.

He lodged initially with a family at the bottom of the 600-foot hill below Dent station. Old Mr Gornall, his daughter and her husband lived there. An evening trip was organised to Morecambe illuminations. Old Mr Gornall joined this, the fare being half a crown. Sandy was on duty when the special returned very late in the day. Old Mr Gornall was not among the passengers. Sandy made inquiries of Hellifield but he had not been seen there. Eventually he landed back next day on a train bound for Hawes. Seemingly he had visited relatives in Morecambe who asked him to stay overnight. He had right enjoyed himself while the family and Sandy were worried sick. Sandy should have charged him excess fare of 7s 6d but it's not easy to do that to someone you are lodging with.

We shall meet Sandy again when the snow dogs howl.

Trouble with farmers

Another aspect of the stationmaster's work was settling claims with farmers whose sheep had met an untimely end on the permanent way.

Jim Taylor, "Well we thought of giving you ten bob."

Farmer, screaming, "What, that was the best ewe in the flock, I want £1."

So, eventually, as they both knew it would be, 15s (75p) was the settlement figure. There was honour to be satisfied on both sides and haggling was par for the course.

One farmer got a shock when heaving an already dead sheep onto the line. It was speedily tossed back by a passing ganger.

Leslie Brown at Garsdale was asked if he could run to get some parcels on a waiting train. "Not for 15s a week" was his retort.

The tale of the teacake

Back again at Horton in Ribblesdale in the days of stationmaster Jim Taylor, prior to his promotion to Settle. The northbound Thames Clyde Express would sometimes be held at the signals when something slower was struggling ahead. Jim would then invariably be found on the platform for, as he put it, "There is always some nit wants to get out wherever the train stops. Being on hand I made sure he or she got back on sharp." One day the dining car attendant stuck his head out to enquire of stationmaster Taylor, "Why are we stopping here?"

Replied Jim, "Well your mates up ahead are doing badly, you'll be away shortly, but haven't you forgotten something?"

"No, don't think so, what's that?"

Jim, with a straight face, "Oh well I'd better tell you then, whenever you stop on block [at the signals] at Horton in Ribblesdale, old tradition decrees that you present the stationmaster, who you will invariably find on the platform, with a toasted teacake."

A present for the stationmaster!

"Eh up, is that right?"

"Of course it is, why do you think I am telling you?"

"Right then, just a minute."

So off he went and in a couple of minutes Jim was presented in due ceremony with a couple of toasted teacakes. The attendant must have told his mates, as ever after when the express was stopped there he was presented with two toasted teacakes.

There was a sequel to this tale many years later when I told my long-time friend George Horner, signalman at that time at Horton about this. "Well the miserable old beggar," he retorted, "he nivver got me a toasted teacake!"

More quarry work

Still at Horton, there used to be a daily lime train to Delaney's quarry which had a rail connection off the northbound platform end leading to some four miles of standard gauge quarry railways operated by a small fleet of industrial locomotives. Seeing the empties safely back into the loading sidings was the stationmaster's responsibility, involving as it did sharp curves plus an adverse gradient.

Jim would relate how the main line locomotive would pull the train of empty wagons well up the line, then at a signal from him would open the regulator before rushing the trucks over the

Delaney's quarry, Horton-in-Ribblesdale, which had its own extensive rail system and industrial locomotives.

Horton quarry shortly before the rail link was lifted.

SETTLE LIMES

Phone SETTLE 917 & 941

T 911

HORTON, LIMEWORKS.

points and round the corner. Sometimes it would stick, so pull out, further up the line then, zizz, back again.

It was not unusual for trucks to come off the rails, one set of points being a firm favourite, Jim quite nonchalantly recounting how they would be re-railed with blocks or just occasionally the Hellifield steam crane.

Cold comfort

During February 1947 a guard based at Hellifield was faced with the macabre task of dealing with two corpses lying in a van in the north bay at Hellifield. "I took them on a train to Hawes Junction from where they were despatched to Hawes by sledge."

Religious fervour

Returning to George Horner, once a month at Ribblehead station a church service would be held. Once the vicar was late so the then young George in his words, "in the spirit of helpfulness", went up to the lectern intoning, "Let us praise God and sing rule fifty-five." That's the one stating that if a train had been stood at a signal for more than five minutes, the fireman was required to go to the signal box and report their presence.

Well, in a good deal less than five minutes the vicar and George's mum and dad entered while he was still at the lectern. George was, as he put it, "admonished very severely, had there been a hole in the floor I should have been swallowed up."

'Let us praise God and sing rule fifty-five.'

Church service at Garsdale station, which like Ribblehead was a religious centre for a scattered upland community.

Chapter Two

Signal Box Tales

Rum things might happen in a lonely box. At Garsdale a ganger made a habit of visiting this lonely outpost before helping himself to a portion of chocolate bar which the signalman took on each shift. This was eventually resolved by the signalman leaving a bar of laxative chocolate which the ganger apparently gleefully accepted doubtless finding it a moving experience. He did not return.

The signalman or woman's lot is often a lonely one not to everyone's taste. Times past it became on occasion more than hectic. Came the 1980s and the line was run down to the state that there were but two service trains each way each day. Signal boxes had likewise seen closure from thirty five to a mere nine between Hellifield and Howe & Co's sidings some five miles east of Carlisle. Even then two-shift working became the norm, boxes being closed during most of the night hours.

Reprieve

Happily, as has been recounted so many times, the line was reprieved to the extent that those nine boxes are now open twenty-four hours, seven days a week. These are all manual boxes worked in the main by mechanical signals and bell codes.

If you do not understand what a manual signal box involves, visit the preserved box adjacent to Settle station open most Saturdays between 10am and 4pm. Although no longer connected to the Settle-Carlisle it still boasts working signals and bells which you can handle yourself. Retired signalman Derek Soames and his assistants hold court here, along with a regular selection of characters, the whole being likened, with some justification, to, 'the Last of the Summer Wine'.

Derek, as already mentioned, spent fifty years on the railway, the last twenty at Settle Junction box which still exists, having recovered a deal of its former importance due to the vast influx of freight traffic. So much so that extra signals known as IBs – intermediate block – have been employed to break up the longer sections, effectively doubling the line's capacity. There is one modern all-electric box at Kirkby Thore near Appleby where gypsum transported as a by-product from in the main Drax power station is used extensively in the production of

Derek Soames in a fitting location, climbing the up repeater signal at Settle Junction where he was signalman for twenty years.

plasterboard.

In fact this is a rail success story. Coal is routed south from Ayrshire over the Settle-Carlisle to power stations in South Yorkshire, North Nottinghamshire and Lancashire, the gypsum being returned north by rail as already mentioned, while some of the finished plasterboard is sent to Scotland (Glasgow) in specially designed rail containers.

Enough of the general picture, let's learn about some of these singular people and what they got up to.

The vast influx of freight traffic onto the Settle-Carlisle has included the transport of gypsum from Drax power station to the works at Kirkby Thore, near Appleby. A class 60 diesel is seen approaching Ais Gill summit with a train of gypsum empties.

A high-speed accident

Derek was rarely alone at Settle Junction, being accompanied by a selection of collie dogs, the one I remember best being Muttley. Should he depart for a call of nature and a bell ring then Muttley howled until acknowledged. At other times he would stand on hind legs at the frame, forelegs on a lever. When they passed on, Muttley and Tyke found quiet resting places adjacent to the box they guarded so often.

Derek recalls being caught by the area manager on an unheralded early morning visit as he sat on the box steps plucking a chicken. A more dramatic occasion was in 1978 when a china clay train jumped the points at the junction spreading its load around the area of the box, apart that is from in its midst a solitary box van carrying explosives. Although not personally on duty at the time of the accident, Derek and his colleagues spent many weeks mopping up the china clay which got everywhere. There were forty-three wagons involved scattered far and wide, so much so that two breakdown cranes attacked the debris, one from Holbeck at the Hellifield end, the other from Carlisle at the Settle side. When the latter had recovered all it was able to reach, it

Derek and his collie dog Muttley inside Settle Junction box. When a bell rang, Muttley would howl until it was acknowledged!

was taken back to Carlisle, south down the West Coast main line then up the Carnforth line via Wennington to attack the remainder from the Giggleswick direction.

Meantime the army nonchalantly cleared the explosives casually tossing boxes of ammunition man to man.

Over the Drag

Training in times past might be unorthodox. When Dickie Birtle started as trainee signalman at Lazonby, he recalled the signalmen's inspector calling once a week to see how he was doing and to ask a few questions.

Like most young lads Dickie enjoyed a night out with his mates. After one such, returning home at 2am, he was back on duty at 6am when Willy Marshall the Scottish inspector called. In the midst of his questions Dickie let out a huge yawn.

Said Willy, "I'm no boring you am I?"

On another occasion he was questioned over his actions about a hypothetical train smash with wagons upside down and scattered all over the shop.

Replied Dickie, "Well Mr Marshall, I think I would go home!"

Near airborne

Dramatic things might happen if as on occasion a train descending the grade went a tad too fast. Such was the case at Stainforth sidings where a box long since closed suffered two near fatal strikes. The first involved a train of trestle wagons carrying outsize sheet steel. This sheared off the front of the box facing the tracks.

The second event concerned a train of tank wagons, which again travelling over-fast took away a large section of the front including the signalman's bicycle stored underneath. On neither occasion are the signalman's comments recorded, though a strong rumour grew that an ejector seat was to be fitted for the signalman on duty.

During Wold War 2, Tim Hodgson on duty at remote Mallerstang box took off the shield of his motorbike light when returning home in darkness after a long winter night shift. Needless to say a policeman stopped him but eventually let him proceed simply to find his way back home and overdue sleep. One does wonder just what a policeman was doing in Mallerstang, hardly a crime hotspot.

Mishap at Stainforth.

The vulnerable box at Stainforth Sidings.

Laughter at Blea Moor

At Blea Moor, where incidentally the water supply was until recently delivered by the early morning train from Skipton, some odd things occurred.

One signalman, sat on board the chemical toilet while lighting his pipe, dropped the match between his legs but shifted quick when the resulting conflagration set fire to his shirt tail!

This was George Horner's box for many years, shared among others with his father, also George Horner, who amazingly followed his son into the box rather than the other way round. It was George senior who famously on the night of Monday 7 December 1964 called his mate at Dent to ask him to check on the state of the Luton Bathgate car carrier. "Eh up, looks like three of them Humber Snipes is missing." And so they were, blown off the flat trucks in the teeth of the gale and now across the up track on Ribblehead Viaduct. You can read the full story of this in a later chapter.

A regular visitor in times past was Eric Treacy, the Railway Bishop. George junior recalls him entering with "I hope you have got the kettle on George." In those days the Bishop had a universal pass.

A fishy tale

Another signalman at Blea Moor recalled a goods train passing on a really wild night as he changed shift. A van door was not properly secured and blew open. Umpteen boxes full of kippers came flying out. "We should of course have collected and handed these in. In fact we did just that with several, though we kept a few and lived off kippers for weeks!"

The spectacular accident at Settle Junction in 1978 when a china clay train jumped the points and spread its load over a wide area. Two breakdown cranes were required to clear up the devastation.

George Horner, photographed at Wennington box. His many legendary tales invariably involved a refill of his pipe with baccy.

Getting up steam!

George junior is one of those characters that once met you never forgot. I first came across him when he was signalman at Wennington on the branch from Settle Junction to Carnforth. George had suffered a heart attack and so had been moved to a less arduous post more easy of access. When eventually he retired I was invited to visit his home in a bungalow adjacent the Settle-Carlisle at Horton in Ribblesdale. This is where I heard many of his tales, invariably related over a large mug of coffee, a refill of his pipe with baccy and finally the combustion process during which he disappeared for a time rather like a Black Five pulling north out of Hellifield.

A man of immense skill, he was a gifted photographer, an outstanding calligrapher and a builder of the most amazing model carts – in a former life he had been a horseman.

Ask anyone who knew him, his tale-telling was legendary. He gave a deal of thought before starting and no matter how many times you had heard it, it was always a little different.

Trouble with gangers

Take the one about the gangers working on the southbound track in the cutting immediately outside the south portal of Blea Moor Tunnel, the longest on the line. Being summer it was in George's words, "terrible 'ot". Several of the gang had taken off their shirts and left them by the lineside. One fella hung his on a convenient willow bush. The up Thames Clyde Express steam-hauled was due, the linesman blew his hooter and they stood clear. George takes over:

"As the train passed me I looked at it very closely to make sure nothing was amiss and noticed a shirt flapping about in the motion of this engine. So I called Ribblehead and advised them of this, 'Don't be too worried there doesn't appear to be a fella in it.'

Came knocking off time and the gang came strolling back past my box all bar one carrying

Express shirt collection at Blea Moor!   *'Where's thi shirt lad?'*

a shirt over his arm. So I called out to this chap minus his shirt, 'Where's thi shirt lad?'

'I hung it on't t'willow bush by t'line side. T'express came along and githered it up. What I'll tell my missus I don't know.'

'Well it'll not bi t'only shirt thi has, tell her what 'appened.'

'And would your missus believe a story like that?'"

Gales of laughter from George, sometimes it made him cry.

A sheepy story

Another concerned the local sheep. One day the signalmen's inspector dropped by, had a brew and a pipe before remarking to George, "Aren't you going to do something about that sheep in the four foot?" This is between the rails on the northbound line and the Thames-Clyde was due.

"It'll be reet," retorts George. The train arrived at speed, the inspector covered his eyes and at the last possible moment the sheep arose, sauntered out of harm's way then returned after the train had passed. Next week's special train orders arrived with a spare copy 'For the sheep of Blea Moor.'

Lamp replacement

One of the joys of Blea Moor was replacing the oil-filled signal lamps each week. Somewhat like an eight-day clock these allowed some twenty-four hours leeway. George always reckoned the worst to be the down Blea Moor distant signal at the northern end of the viaduct. There were a lot taller signals but not many atop a near hundred foot embankment. Said George, "You would get up top with the lamp and damn me, the wind blew it out. Come down, find a bit of shelter – not easy just there – then relight it. Sometimes you had to have three or four attempts and boy it could be both wet and windy – not to say terrifying."

The following poem exemplifies the difficulties in relighting a signal lamp:

THE MATCH BOX
By Sir Gar

The night is dark and stormy,
The rain is pouring down.
The 'Starting' light has just gone out,
No doubt the wick is drowned.

The 'Boat Train' is not far away,
It's racing through the storm.
There must not be a slight delay
Or check of any form.

If the 'Distant' is at caution,
Two minutes will be booked.
Control will say, "Now please explain,
This can't be overlooked."

So, on goes my railway mac,
Now one in every FOUR.
It should be one in every THREE
Just as it was before.

And out I go into the night,
Through the soaking rain.
To light the 'Starting' signal lamp,
And save delay to train.

Having reached the signal,
I climb towards the sky.
The thing is shaking like a leaf,
And me right up on high.

And with my box of matches,
And hand lamp in my hand,
I try to light the 'ruddy' thing,
High up above the land.

I've used two dozen matches,
My hand lamp has gone out.
My cap has blown right off my head,
A wintry gale, no doubt.

At last I have succeeded,
But forty matches 'gone.'
I make my tracks towards the earth,
With one hand hanging on.

Back into the cabin,
To the failure of the 'Block.'
This is far too much for me,
Roll on 'Six o'clock'

NB: The reference to 'FOUR should be every THREE' relates to the railway mac, the issue of which was cut back from every three years to four.

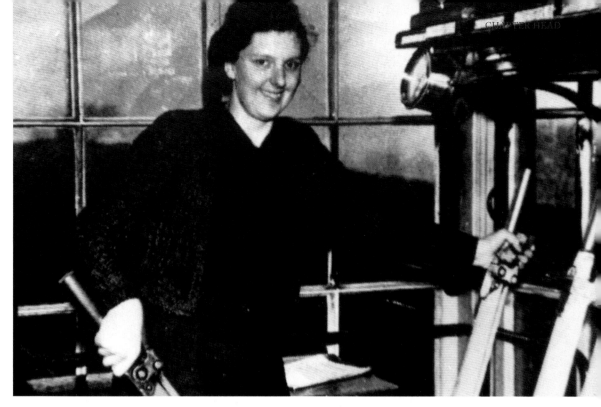

Inside Selside box, which during World War 2 was exclusively manned by women.

'Come on, get 'em off!'

A risqué tale

Below Ribblehead and splitting up the section between there and Horton in Ribblesdale there used to be a signal box at Selside. It was a simple affair with no points, just up and down distant and home signals. During World War 2 it was manned exclusively by women. One day a northbound freight was stopped there overlong. The crew were on mileage work so were anxious to get moving. Fireman Jimmy Fishwick under rule fifty-five approached the bottom of the steps, calling out to the signalwoman a'top them, "Come on, get 'em off", referring to the pegs – signals. She thought he meant something else, slapped his face and reported him.

Husband and wife Kit and Edith Sedgewick were for a time at Horton and Selside boxes respectively and on the same shift. Kit on watching a northbound freight pass sent seven bells to Edith, "Stop and examine", following this with a telephone explanation, "There is something hanging out."

Shortly he received the following reply, "Silly old devil our Kit, it's only a cow's tail!"

The sequel to this was when Control enquired as to why a train had been stopped due to a cow's tail hanging out. Kit soon sorted that, "You'd want to get your tail back inside were it hanging out all the way to Carlisle." No more was heard about that incident.

Fruit salad

Another tale concerned Derek Soames at Settle Junction and George Horner on relief at Selside. Bananas used to be shipped into Barry Docks from where special trains with steam-heated vans ripened the fruit as it travelled around the country. On this particular day such a train was slowly threading Settle Junction when Derek noticed a giant hand of bananas lodged on the roof of a van. It had clearly been dropped there by a crane and stuck against a ventilator. This was too good an opportunity to miss, the train was making slow progress following another freight block by block. Derek rang George on the circuit telephone knowing that Selside box, where he was on relief was very close to the down track yet standing quite high.

"George, have you got a long pole to catch a hand of bananas on the roof of the special, its only travelling slowly?"

"Aye, the window cleaning pole has a brush attached, I'll see what I can do."

He was sick of bananas by the weekend.

More problems with ammunition

When Bill Mitchell was editor of the *Dalesman* magazine they had an employee Dick Clark who carried out many odd jobs. Dick had been a signalman at Helwith Bridge which served the Foredale quarries through a triangular junction. He rode out there on his bike from Settle day in day out.

During World War 2 some trucks broke away from an ammunition train travelling north near Ribblehead station. Word of course spread like wildfire from one signal box to another. According to Dick, he stood as it were on the burning deck as these trucks full of ammunition hurtled by.

In fact Bill later learned that Dick didn't stay in the signal box but ran like hell to "top o't field"!

Setting up shop

Over the summit there were equally bizarre occurrences. Alan Dugdale of Langwathby told of his dad during the latter days of World War 2 in Kirkby Stephen box. Being out in the country it was still possible to get hold of some foodstuffs. He put up a large notice on the signal box door, "Rabbits and eggs." In his words trains would stop and back up, "I'll just have a couple of rabbits Andy, can you get us some for Thursday?"

"One day I had an express stop, 'Food is getting terrible scarce in Leeds, can you get us as much as you can? I'll be back on Thursday. Don't worry about the guard, I'll square him.'

I think I got him three dozen eggs and half a dozen rabbits. I was buying eggs at 2s 3d a dozen and selling them at 4s 6d – 'and here's 10s for yourself and don't forget, as many as you can.' It was a damned good thing."

At Dent Station box Jack Sedgwick had a nice little earner – a spot of haircutting.

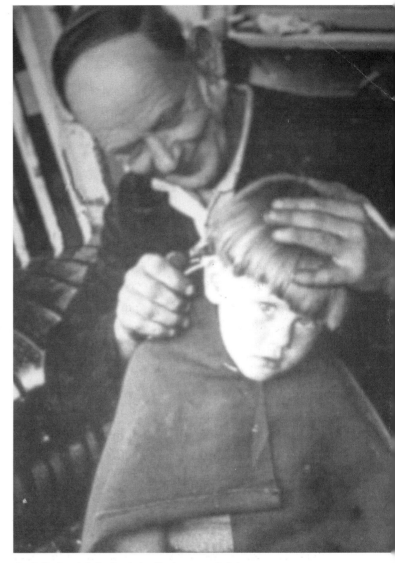

Jack Sedgwick had a 'nice little earner' doing a spot of haircutting at Dent Station box.

Rabbits and eggs at Kirkby Stephen.

Fire!

Dickie Birtle recalls when Bob Turnbull was signalman at Lazonby and the box caught fire. He dashed out before remembering it was pay day, his wage packet having been delivered and still in his jacket pocket. So he rushed back for it, collecting for good measure the signal box clock. This was in the days of coal-fired stoves.

Dickie had his second stint as a signalman in the box at Low House Crossing after several years at a different post on the railways. After two days with the regular signalman, inspector Willy Marshall called to see if he was competent to take over:

"'Hang on,' I said, 'I've only been here two days.'

'Never mind,' says Willy, 'we will just have a walk out.'

So we walked down the trackside to Armathwaite and back – near four miles, the while Willy firing questions at me.

On our return and climbing the box steps he was picking my brains on 'Stop and examine'. He turned round, said, 'I think you will be alright', and that was that."

Jimmy Richardson did forty-five years on the railway, thirty-nine on the Settle-Carlisle of which twenty seven were in Culgaith box. This was during the 1950/60s when steam was still king. One day a car went off the skew bridge between Culgaith and Langwathby. It landed on the railway. He advised Control at Carlisle, the line was stopped and trains diverted over the West Coast Main Line thence via Tebay and Ingleton to Settle Junction.

The vehicle was eventually and unbelievably driven off under its own power via a farmer's accommodation crossing. After the Great Heck accident on the East Coast Main Line the local authority covering Culgaith put up crash barriers to prevent a recurrence yet ignored the actual spot where not one but two vehicles had taken to the rails.

IT COULD HAPPEN TO YOU

By "Roja"

Across the shiny frame he lay,

His face a mask of pain.

He was breathing his last as the postal went past,

And he tried to give 'section' in vain.

For he fell as he reached for the little black key,

As he passed out he sighed with regret,

"I've so much to lose – some passes to use,

And I've not had my holidays yet."

His mate stopped the postal and yelled to the guard,
"Loose working! This really won't do.
Go back with your train, and start over again,
For I haven't had section from you."

Then he rang back the junction and got no reply,
And cursed as in anger he said,
"You're worse than Control, you should be on the dole
One would actually think you were dead."

Then he hauled out his bike and flew up the line,
And he found his mate dead where he lay,
So he took a quick look, put his name in the book,
And phoned the Control right away.

The Controller lay down his tea with regret,
And grumbled, "I hope it's not true;
It's a bit of a bore, are you really quite sure?
His day isn't up until two."

"But I'll send you a doctor as soon as I can
(If you're lucky, by tea time on Monday);
In the meantime you'd better explain in a letter
Why the man couldn't wait until Sunday."

When the doctor arrived and examined the corpse,
He cried, "It's beyond all belief!
A lavatory pan might have saved this poor man,
Who died while awaiting relief!"

A kid's tale

During the 1950s Derek Soames spent time as a signalman at Long Preston between Settle Junction and Hellifield. In those days near everything travelled by rail – goods, animals, whatever. One day he was approached in the box by John Hall the stationmaster.

"Now then Derek, have you ever milked a goat?"

"No," replied Derek, "but I have milked cows before."

"Well," went on the stationmaster, "a goat has just arrived by rail from St Ives – not sure whether its Cambs or Cornwall but it's a long way and this goat needs milking, it's in agony. Its eventually to be taken on by road to Tosside. Now if I bring it down to the box will you milk it?"

So Derek replied that he would. As luck would have it he had a trainee signalman with him who was just about ready to take on the job, so he left him in charge and milked the goat.

This took place in the goods yard where the goat drank water from a fire bucket while Derek worked away at the other end. They reckon goat milk to be the most pure milk available yet no one else would drink it so Derek polished off the lot.

Life on two wheels

Ken Harper recalls Charlie Rae who was a Scot. In LMS days each part of the country was split into promotional areas, so you might move from Scotland to England and back within the same promotion area. Charlie was born and joined the railway in Dumfriesshire, moved to Crosby Garrett as signalman and stopped there. During the 1940/50s the box was on the down Carlisle-bound side.

If you were lucky you had a motorbike as transport, cars being for the aristocracy. Charlie had a push bike, moreover a push bike with a puncture. He had it upside down in the four-foot lie-by siding outside the box while carrying out a repair. He took on a train from Kirkby Stephen, 'train entering section' and almost immediately got a bell 1 5 5, 'shunt train to allow following train to pass.'

So up in the box he left the signal on to stop the first train. It cleared the points into the siding and halted. Charlie indicated to the train crew to reverse into the siding, set the points and cleared the ground signal to set back inside, only then noticing the guard hanging over from the rear of his van beneath the veranda frantically trying to hook the bike from the four-foot with his shunting pole as the train reversed inside. He didn't succeed.

The trouble with cranes

Back to George Horner junior on duty at Blea Moor when he received a 'stop and examine' call from Ribblehead. This was followed by the news that a crane jib was swinging around fast and loose.

George had an up goods due to pass so to be on the safe side routed this into the up loop. The fireman from this, quickly followed by his driver, entered the box demanding to know why they were being held up as they were on mileage work.

George did his best to placate them before the down freight came slowly into view. Now cranes should always be run with the jib pointing in the opposite direction to that of travel. This was not the case in this instance, the jib having broken loose of its securing point and swinging wildly in a great arc.

George remembers the train crew in his box watching events, their mouths dropping further and further until the driver exclaimed, "Wow, that jib would have opened us up like a can of sardines had it made contact."

Having put the offending train into the down loop and advised Control, George reminded the crew in his box that the signalman is there to protect them, not deliberately delay them. Ever after, if they were stopped at Blea Moor they would pop in for a crack, or, more often rattling through, give a cheery wave and crow from the whistle.

Waste not, want not

While Derek Soames was a signalman at Long Preston between Hellifield and Settle, and living at the latter, there was a degree of rationalisation taking place including the demolition of surplus station buildings, many in Lancashire. Near Heysham Harbour, there was a tip into which much of this material found its way. Ballast, stone and sleepers made up many trainloads which were routed up the old Lancashire & Yorkshire line through Hellifield and then down what is now known as the Dales Branch through Giggleswick, Wennington, Lancaster Green Ayre and so to Heysham.

It got to the stage at times when trains were refused at Heysham as they could not cope with the influx of traffic. On one such occasion a train load of wagons was put into the sidings at Long Preston awaiting a path. Derek noticed that one wagon was full of stone setts, the type used on roads in station yards. Now the stationmaster at Settle, Jim Taylor, was as previously recounted keen on gardening. Derek knowing him well, rang him up.

"Jim, I have a wagon load of stone setts bound for Heysham tip, just wondered if they might be of any use for your gardens?"

"Whoa, don't you let them go Derek."

"Well there is a wagon load of sleepers too Jim, could you do with them as firewood?"

"Tell you what Derek, get the pick-up goods to collect both wagons and drop them off here, I will square it all up."

So next morning Derek was there early, stopped the pick-up which usually ran as far as Garsdale, sometimes Appleby, and got them to pick up both wagons. You can see in the picture on page 44 the garden Jim and his colleagues built on the site of the present car park to the rear of the Settle Station booking hall during the 1960s. No record exists of the fate of the sleepers.

Imagine trying to do something like this now. There would have had to have been an Act of Parliament with the obligatory two-year review. Health and Safety would have been involved and perhaps required acknowledgement. In those days, if something surplus was available and required, then you just got on with it.

The garden at Settle station with its stone setts, which Jim Taylor obtained from a train at Long Preston courtesy of Derek Soames.

Moonlighting

Two more tales from Dickie Birtle, the first at Long Marton where stationmaster Dickie Harper used to play holy hell with him for wearing ice blue jeans which were all the rage at the time. The railway uniform trousers of the day were akin to wearing coal sacks. Dickie Birtle cracked it by having the uniform trousers to hand and pulling them over his jeans when he saw the stationmaster approaching.

Again regarding the two Dickies, stationmaster Harper had a sideline as an antiques dealer. Many railway employees had a second string to their bow, remuneration not being over generous. He persuaded Dickie Birtle to earn a bob or two polishing brasses, (using railway brasso) at two bob a time. This was fine when your wage was around £7 per week. It lost all its attraction when one day he was faced with a damned great elephant which took weeks to clean.

A Grizeburn signalman was a dab hand at making sticks and shepherds' crooks, while at Ormside Frank Ridding was also a cobbler. Drivers in the know would sling off a pair of shoes with a note, "Back on the 10.55am." It cost 12s 6d for soling and heeling. Further north at Little

Salkeld a signalman had a large apple orchard. In season these were in great demand. Another bred fell ponies. All of this was hidden from the inspector who probably knew what was going on, though so long as it did not interfere with railway work would turn a blind eye. Wages were low in remote signal boxes and one had to make ends meet.

Tommy Harden, a signalman at Long Preston, was chatting to another on the phone one day when he became very agitated as he opened his salary envelope. "I've cracked it, I've cracked it," he chorused.

"What have you done?" asked his mate.

"I've got to double figures, including much overtime, topped ten pounds!"

Company!

When Derek Soames was on relief at Hellifield North box one cold winters evening in the early sixties, he was due on duty at a minute past midnight. The box was switched out prior to midnight so he would have the fire to light. Coming up the subway he was conscious of someone huddled on a seat. He passed the time of day with a lady, enquiring what she was doing there, sat in darkness.

"I've been potholing and had a lift here and been told to wait for the Glasgow train."

"Well that's not 'til 3.15am, the night sleeper from St. Pancras, you'll be frozen." Thinking quickly, "Now don't get me wrong, I am going on duty and there will soon be a grand fire and some hot tea, I'm not begging you to come into the box, it's up to you."

So of course she accepted and Derek obviously knew when to tell her to get back to the platform. Last he saw of her was a hand waving from the train.

A fortnight later, Tuesday market day in Settle, and this same lass rushed up to Derek, gave him a big hug, then was gone.

He doesn't recall telling his wife this tale.

Last rites

One more from Derek who also had another string to his bow. Arriving for afternoon shift at Settle Junction, he was confronted by the signalmen's inspector with: "Well I've seen folk walk to get on shift, I've seen 'em arrive by motorbike or pushbike and many a time bi car. But never ever have I seen someone arrive by hearse in full funereal attire." Derek had this sideline for over thirty years.

Finally another tale of moonlighting. This nameless signalman would ring up the roster clerk to enquire as to whether he might do a swap next Wednesday to attend a funeral. There were several similar requests until the clerk sussed that the signalman was making money on the side as a gravedigger for not just one church but six! In his limited free time he was also the local chimney sweep.

Chapter Three

A Walk on the Wild Side

Derek Soames recounts two rather different stories from his younger days:

The Short Walk

Nigel Mussett was very keen on both railways and plant life. I knew Nigel well and arranged a walking permit for the two of us up the 'Drag.' On one occasion we drove up to Dent by car, then set off to walk to the water troughs in Garsdale through Rise Hill Tunnel. I knew what the position was over this, so rang Garsdale signal box to find out if any traffic was due.

There wasn't any so we set off and walked through Rise Hill Tunnel out to the troughs. Nigel recorded the indigenous plant life, something not possible now, walking permits not being available.

The Long Walk

Back in 1975 our eldest son Michael was at Loughborough University. Having some free time out of term I asked him how he fancied walking to Carlisle.

"Aye," he replied. "Why not?"

So I had a word with the area manager at Preston stressing that I did not want any restrictions on the walk. Eventually he agreed that we might do it. I had to sign a document to say that I was responsible for my son, so there was no comeback if anything went amiss.

So, on 9 April 1975 we set off from Settle station collecting all the signatures of all the signalmen we met in their boxes on the way. The details follow the end of this chapter. Note that some appear more than once, where a relief signalman had been on duty at different boxes on consecutive dates.

The first day we walked from Settle to Garsdale, sleeping in the platelayers' bothy, actually the up side waiting room on the station. When we arrived there I mentioned to Michael not seeing his camera. Well, we were not able to find it, indicating that we might have left it in a signal box. We tried contacting the various boxes we had passed but without success.

In the event we remembered that as we came into Garsdale from Rise Hill Tunnel it was snowing very hard so we sheltered in a platelayers' cabin for a while. When we set off again Michael had forgotten his camera. So we had a word with the signalman at Ais Gill who was a Dent lad. He very kindly agreed to pick us up at 6am next morning and take us across the Coal

Derek Soames and his elder son Michael set off from Settle station in April 1975 to walk the length of the line to Carlisle.

The signatures of all the signalmen met during the 72-mile walk. Some of them appear more than once due to being on relief work on another shift.

Road over the top of the tunnel back to Dent Station so that we might walk that stretch again. Sure enough his camera was in the cabin, so we walked it again from Dent to Garsdale before we set off that day over Ais Gill. The end of day two landed us at Appleby where we decided to look for bed and breakfast and a degree of comfort.

Our third day took us as far as Armathwaite. I used to know the lads in the

Control office in Carlisle, one of whom had been the stationmaster at Armathwaite. So I found where the key was for Armathwaite box, it not being regularly open. With this I got into the box, rang my mate and asked him, did he know where we might get bed and breakfast?

He explained where to go to, Mr and Mrs So and So. He used to be a signalman and take in bed and breakfast. So off we went down into Armathwaite, knocked at this door only to find the lady had stopped taking B&B some time back. I explained who I was and what we were doing.

"Oh yes, I remember So and So, used to be Stationmaster here, come on in, I'll fix you up."

So we had a bed with a proper feather mattress. We had a right grand

Journey's end at Petteril Bridge Junction, Carlisle.

meal too. I remember that my toes had been banging on the sleeper ends so many times that both my big toes had bruised and the nails were coming off. She found me some tape and bound my toe nails back on again.

The following day we walked the eight miles into Carlisle where Willie Marshall, the signalmen's inspector, met us at Petteril Bridge and walked us into Carlisle station over the multiplicity of tracks.

Well, I had a free pass to come back with, but Michael hadn't, so he went to walk through the barrier to the booking office. His ticket was demanded. "No," replied Michael, "I haven't come on the train, just walked it from Settle."

We had to get Willie Marshall to vouch that we had in fact done just that.

So Michael eventually got a ticket. I had tried to get a cab pass to ride back in the cab of the diesel pulling the express but it was turned down. Anyway, I spoke to the driver while he was stood in Carlisle station and told him the tale. He dare not let us climb aboard there but told us to get into the first coach so that when we got to Appleby we might join him there, which is what happened.

When we got off at Settle we had to walk down home. I was walking with little short steps, every sixty-foot length of rail having twenty-four sleepers. Me being over six foot, I normally take big strides but had to adjust to short ones for the duration of our trek.

A high-life contrast

This involved the author.

Not so long ago, at twenty-fours hours notice, I was asked to act as train manager on a charter special along with two colleagues. This charter though was something out of the ordinary. It was a private charter for a large national firm whose top employees were on a week's course in the Dales.

The owner chartered the train for just sixty, the arrangement being that there would be two first class pullmans plus a kitchen car from which morning coffee and delicatessen would be served and later afternoon tea. In the event the full rake of pullmans arrived, seemingly as the batteries needed charging up. A Class 37 diesel supplied traction.

After coffee the champagne flowed which my two colleagues and self were invited to sample. It was up to scratch. At Armathwaite the company detrained to join two vintage buses, 1949/51 as I recall. We cadged a lift. They visited a local hotel for prearranged lunch while we three, plus the two bus drivers, had lunch at another hostelry.

This was early March. On the return journey the scenery was at its most spectacular, plastered in snow. Sadly many of the guests had by then fallen asleep.

Nancy Dawson and her two older sisters – the Blea Moor railway children.

Nancy's dad, John Dawson, who in 1939 accepted the subganger's post at Blea Moor and moved his family into one of the railway cottages.

Chapter Four

Life at Blea Moor

On one of my many visits to George Horner's home, he mentioned someone that knew a deal more about Blea Moor and the railway than he. Intrigued, I prompted him for more information. It turned out that the lady concerned actually lived in the same village as me and I had known her for years without being aware of her connection with the railway. So I approached Nancy Edmondson and arranged to interview her accompanied by Bill Mitchell who wanted a video record. The venue was to be our best room, transformed into a studio. I had my audio recording gear set up, likewise Bill his video.

Nancy was perhaps understandably intimidated by all this so I decided to open a bottle of wine to, as it were, 'break the ice'. No sooner done than Bill uptipped the bottle of red over what fortunately was a red patterned carpet. The ice was broken. Nancy laughed for several minutes before recounting her amazing story which bears echoes of the Railway Children yet with one difference – it is fact – not fiction.

"We were not really railway children to start with; indeed I was born at Scow House near Cowgill in Dentdale, though my elder sisters, Margaret and Edith, respectively eight and eleven years my senior were initially brought up at Salt Lake Cottages, south of Ribblehead. Our parents, John (Jack) Stainton and Lucy Dawson, had married during 1921, dad originally being a farmer at Chapel House, Chapel le Dale, but having to leave home as there were too many mouths to feed from too little income. He turned to the erstwhile Midland Railway where a cousin had already found employment.

During 1939 Dad was offered and accepted the subganger's post at Blea Moor on the Settle-Carlisle line. The attraction was a tied property. No 1 Blea Moor Cottages was one of a pair of traditional steep-eaved Midland cottages, the likes of which were erected the length and breadth of its empire for its servants. There was also a more modern detached house built next to the present signal box. It is still in situ and presently occupied.

We moved in prior to Christmas 1939. Dad's length was from midway through Blea Moor tunnel to the southern end of Ribblehead Viaduct, from 500 feet below the moor to the exposed extremity of the viaduct 104 feet above it."

Basic facilities

Nancy's new home was rudimentary yet comfortable. "Water was supplied to a wash-house adjacent to the cottages from the same source which fed the huge water tank used to replenish thirsty locomotives. Coal came courtesy of firemen's shovels to feed the fire in the kitchen-cum-

The pigsty at Blea Moor – also useful for sunbathing.

The Blea Moor toilet was a mite drafty.

living room. The sitting room was used only for best – when there were visitors. Lighting was by paraffin lamps and candles. I shudder now to think of reading in bed, a candle balanced on my pillow. We were self-sufficient for eggs and bacon, though milk had to be collected from Winterscales Farm, some quarter of a mile distant, a pretty enough walk in spring, though less attractive through several feet of snow.

On Tuesdays mother would go to Settle shopping, catching the pick-up slow train at Ribblehead. It also ran on Saturdays. Quite often she would be dropped off at Blea Moor when returning, provided the crew knew her. There was no platform, descent to rail level involving a considerable jump. Bulk supplies were delivered, by rail of course, once a month from T.D. Smith's in Settle.

Our toilet was a primitive affair, an earth closet at the bottom of the garden. At night we took a candle sheltered by the ladling can, really just an enamelled jug used for supplying our coal-fired boiler from buckets carried from the wash-house. The WC was a mite draughty, paper not always staying in the right spot. Later we were provided with a chemical toilet at which Dad scoffed, 'Them as use 'em can empty 'em', promptly departing for a local pothole. I never was keen on that sport."

Schooling

"Schooling involved a 1¼ mile walk to Ribblehead, from where a bus took us to Chapel le Dale School. For a time Mum was a teacher at the same school. Margaret and I would load the hems of our waterproofs with small stones in an effort to prevent us from becoming airborne as we walked beneath the viaduct. We would often shelter behind a pier prior to making a dash for it during a lull in the gale. Frequently and against the rules, we would walk across the viaduct

Weighing down waterproofs to avoid being blown away.

The school bus coming over Sleights.

where, due to our lack of inches, it was surprisingly sheltered. There were refuges provided for the gangers in which you might take cover in the event of a passing train.

Later Margaret lodged in Settle during the week while at the high school, returning on Friday. In due course I too travelled to Settle High, though by this time a school bus was provided, either a Guy or Daimler 35-seater. Dave, the driver, would blow his horn coming up Sleights above the Hill Inn, from where he might see me crossing the viaduct. I knew then to hurry for the pick up point at Ribblehead. Once, north of Salt Lake Cottages, we ran into a huge drift, Dave having to reverse right back to Ribblehead, leaving me to return home very early, again via the viaduct."

Dad spent the winter digging out the points.

Mountains of snow

"Thinking of snow inevitably brings to mind the winter of 1947. This was a time of mountains of the stuff but also long strong rays of sunlight; in many ways a very pretty winter, the few trees frozen into fantastic patterns with their ice-laden branches. Father spent that winter fighting a losing battle to keep the points clear of ice, coming home with eyebrows and whiskers frozen into icicles.

Beyond our house lay a cutting prior to the tunnel, this being blocked solid with a snowplough jammed in its midst for good measure. We were not entirely cut off as the signal box was still in touch with the outside world. Through the signalman we learned that a revolutionary snowblower was coming to clear this and other cuttings on the way. Everyone was advised to stay indoors as there would be snow everywhere and it might be dangerous. We went upstairs to watch while dad went outside and sat on the rail full of confidence that it would not appear. 'It'll niver get up 'ere' was his laconic observation, being fully justified for the jet engine mounted on a flat truck went straight into the first minor drift and itself became stuck. Eventually Italian POWs dug it out by hand and it disappeared whence it came.

During this time the 'pick-up' was of course unable to get through from Garsdale so we rode down to Settle in the snowplough, pushed before the engine. Perhaps I should explain that these ploughs were monster items being the full height of a locomotive and mounted on their own wheels. A train was formed of plough, a six-wheeled locomotive, brake van, another similar locomotive facing the opposite direction and a further plough, thus allowing for tackling drifts in either direction. A ride on, or rather in the plough was not so unusual to us; after all we seemed to ride most places on locomotives. Towards the end of my sixteen years at Blea Moor I used to visit my sister Edith by then working in Newcastle. Returning from Garsdale the crew were old friends, stopping the train at Blea Moor rather than having me walk the 1¼ miles from Ribblehead on a wild day.

This was fairly typical of S & C practice, the line being something of a law unto itself, not through any feeling of malice towards higher authority, rather simply a matter of adapting to meet the extremes of weather and terrain through which it ran.

Dave, the bus driver, told me of great concern for the safety of the viaduct during the war years. He recalls the Home Guard, equipped at that stage only with shotguns, riding on the running boards of cars bound for Ribblehead, brandishing their weapons a la Chicago. Later more normally provided with rifles, sentries patrolled the viaduct from boxes provided at either end, apparently oblivious to possible fifth column activities a hundred feet below.

The other properties were tenanted by railwaymen, William Davidson living in the detached house for a time. A lay preacher, he regularly pushed his bike through the near two-mile-long tunnel to appointments in Dentdale. We had lodgers in the shape of Arthur Lamb, whose wife still lives in Hellifield, Arthur Stevenson and Jack Cowperthwaite. The Horners, both called George, were signalmen on the Blea Moor roster though they lived elsewhere. George junior provided social evenings for a time on the up platform at Ribblehead station. It seems hard to believe now but we had some wonderful happy hours dancing there to sounds from his early record player. We regularly had additional lodgers, some at unexpectedly short notice when the weather clammed in."

Married from Blea Moor

"Our Edith must have set some sort of record on her wedding day, leaving home, hair still in curlers, wedding dress over her arm, bridal transport courtesy of a Midland 0-6-0 freight locomotive brought to an unscheduled halt at the signals. One wonders what the crew were thinking as they deposited her at Ribblehead. She changed into her finery at the Station Inn prior to the wedding at Chapel le Dale Church. The reception was back at the Station Inn. Few brides can have embarked on such a start to their wedding day.

Sister Margaret went one better. Married to Bob Hadaway, signalman at Ribblehead, they lived in the detached house at Blea Moor. Going into labour unexpectedly early, her husband's Blea Moor colleague stopped the up Thames Clyde Express. The guard pulled and tugged, Bob and our dad pushed and shoved and several passengers lent a hand. And that just to get her into a carriage! Later an ambulance met the express at Settle to effect the transfer to Cawderghyll Maternity Hospital, Skipton, where in due course a son was born sound in wind and limb."

Sister Edith's bridal transport – a goods engine!

Changed into wedding finery at the Station Inn.

Hard labour – stopping the express for sister Margaret.

Train smash

Possibly the most momentous event to befall Blea Moor was the train smash on 18 April 1952, the background to which is as follows: The 9.15am from Glasgow, the up Thames Clyde Express, was formed of ten coaches headed by 4-6-0 No 46117 'Welsh Guardsman', this in turn being piloted by the ex Midland 4-4-0 Compound No 41040. This entourage passed a permanent way gang at the northern end of the tunnel, they noticing that something was amiss with the pilot engine, yet were powerless to give a warning. In fact, the near side brake rod on the compound's tender was flailing around amidst the ballast as the train headed into the tunnel at about 50mph. There are loops with facing points at Blea Moor and here matters came to a head. The pilot engine safely negotiated the point-work but its wild appendage struck the point operating mechanism, moving the blades under the second engine and coaches.

Let Nancy resume her story:

"I was thirteen by then and, on a balmy April day, sunbathing on top of the pigsty. This was in the corner of the garden adjacent the lineside with a clear view towards the tunnel. It would be 200 yards from the facing points at the north end of the loop. I heard the express approaching

Royal Scot class 46117 'Welsh Guardsman' on its side at Blea Moor.
Opposite: Aerial view of Blea Moor after the disastrous derailment of the up Thames-Clyde Express on 18 April .

Presentation of the watch inscribed 'Nancy Dawson, Blea Moor, 18.4.52'. It is still going!

followed by the most almighty crash. Sitting up, I watched spellbound as the second locomotive toppled as though in slow motion onto its side. Three carriages reared up before crashing back sideways over the running lines. Steam was everywhere. Other than the signalman who immediately summoned help, there was just Mum and I on the scene. Mum put on the kettles while I rushed up to the wreckage and found a baby still in its carry-cot which had clearly come through a window. Soon a distressed lady claimed it and they were reunited.

One boy about my own age had very badly lacerated legs after falling through a window. Our home became a casualty clearing station. It was some time before a fleet of relief vehicles arrived at Winterscales, the nearest road access. When the rescuers eventually arrived, they were appalled to find bodies littering the embankment but relieved when they turned out to be passengers who, having done all they could to assist, had taken to sunbathing. The British really are a phlegmatic race. Later still the heavy lifting cranes arrived to clear the wreckage. Mum burst into tears when our young casualty thanked her for tea and biscuits; we heard later that he made a full recovery.

Casualties were thankfully light, the train being nowhere near full and, more particularly, formed of modern steel stock which preserved the essential framework. Still, it was an eerie experience to later pass the remains, covered by flapping tarpaulins in the evening breeze.

When things settled down the Railways Board made me a presentation of a watch at school, which I still have and is still going. It is inscribed, 'Nancy Dawson, Blea Moor, 18.4.52'.

Well-deserved letter from the Chief Commissioner of Girl Guides for England.

> **THE GIRL GUIDES ASSOCIATION**
> (INCORPORATED BY ROYAL CHARTER)
>
> PRESIDENT:
> HER ROYAL HIGHNESS THE PRINCESS ROYAL
>
> IMPERIAL HEADQUARTERS:
> 17-19, BUCKINGHAM PALACE ROAD,
> LONDON, S.W.I.
>
> TELEPHONES: VICTORIA 6001.
> TELEGRAMS: GIRGUIDUS, SOWEST, LONDON
> CODE: 5 LETTER WESTERN UNION.
>
> 19th May, 1952
>
> Dear Nancy,
>
> I want to send you congratulations on your grand reaction to an emergency on the occasion of the train smash. I have heard how well you kept your head and helped continuously in every way you could for as long as help was needed, and I realise that this called for considerable self-control in face of the frightening circumstances with which you were confronted.
>
> We at Headquarters like to think that Guide training will produce the sort of people who rise to the occasion like this, and your action is a fine example to Guides everywhere.
>
> Yours sincerely,
>
> *Mid Burnham.*
>
> Chief Commissioner for England

The Board of School Governors sent me a letter and I also received a similar one from the Chief Commissioner of Girl Guides for England. Mum received recompense for refreshments, sheets and hot-water bottles.

In 1956 Dad retired and we had to relinquish our cottage, moving to Wilshaw near Gearstones, where Mum and he spent many more happy years. Shortly afterwards I left school and started work on Tyneside."

Epilogue

"I still have dreams about the railway. From time to time people were killed on the line either by intent or accident. Dad had taken me into the tunnel as a little girl and one nightmare is of running, running with the train gaining on me as I try to reach daylight. I also think back to when a royal train was due and Dad was detailed to climb the fell and inspect the ventilation shafts to ensure nobody tried to drop anything several hundred feet onto the train. This I have to admit, twenty years after his death, was a duty he shirked, not being much of a royalist.

I no longer live quite so close to the railway which had such an influence on my early years, but one thing did happen as a direct result of it. Remember Dave, the school bus driver? Well, now he's my husband."

Chapter Five

Drama on the Footplate

A stranger on the footplate

The crew walking down the length of the train noticed that Bill was the only passenger, the driver remarking, "Eh lad tha' looks lonely, come along with us and have a ride in the cab."

Nancy Edmondson was not the only one to take unscheduled rides on locomotives. Bill Mitchell recounts that during his early days on the *Dalesman* magazine, transport was very often of the public variety.

On assignment to Wensleydale he had to change to the local train at Garsdale. The line from there as far as Hawes was part of the Midland Empire being contract number five built as a branch of the Settle-Carlisle Railway. At Hawes it made an end-on junction with the North Eastern line from Northallerton. This is the line

The Garsdale branch engine.

now in part operated by the Wensleydale Railway, its avowed intent being to reinstate through running between Northallerton and Garsdale.

In point of fact everyone on that journey rode in the locomotive cab – driver, fireman, guard and Bill. He remembers at each station the stationmaster coming out of his office, noting the absence of passengers, shrugging his shoulders and retreating whence he came. Would that it were possible to move the clock back sixty years.

A runaway!

More dramatically, around 1962/63 Mickey Venn was fireman on a mineral train to Carlisle Kingmoor. Starting from Leeds, Mickey and his driver had taken over at Hellifield. They had several hundred tons of locomotive coal behind mainly in loose-coupled wagons, that is to say

Mickey Venn and driver Hughie Bullock on the front of 9F 92167.

they had little additional braking other than from the brake van at the rear of the train.

Beyond Ais Gill, it rapidly became apparent that the locomotive braking, and that in the first few wagons fitted with continuous brake plus the brake van, was insufficient to hold the train. Driver Gordon Bowers was popping the whistle as they passed Mallerstang signal box to warn of their plight, having already passed the distant signal against them.

Mickey takes over: "Approaching Kirkby Stephen, Gordon instructed me to climb onto the lower locomotive step and jump. This I was loath to do even when Gordon threatened to boot me off before following.

In the event, beyond Kirkby Stephen near Crosby Garrett there is a stretch of level track where we started to slow down, the guard having his brake screwed hard down. Gordon put our engine carefully into reverse and we came to a halt.

Later it was revealed that the fitter recently servicing the engine in Leeds had been called away in a rush as his wife was dangerously ill. Nobody had thought to check on his work, as a result the locomotive being despatched minus a full set of brakes on its left side. The road through Skipton is relatively level, the train being stopped at Hellifield without difficulty to change crews. It might have been a deal worse."

Bill Addy on memories of firing in wild weather

"I've fired locos over the Drag wearing mi' heavy railway mac. The temperature of the fire is 3,500 degrees or something – thirty-five what number – yet there has been ice on the bucket eight feet away!

In torrential rain you don't want it washing all the muck down to shovel on the fire. On big engines, 'Crabs' and the like, the fire 'ole door slides with one handle which the driver opens. You sling in the coal and hopefully not too much slurry and he shuts it, his hand encased in an oily rag. You don't want no cold air getting in either."

Loose livestock

Driver Bill (Dakes) Dakin stopped his freight train outside Kirkby Stephen signal box. The signalman slid open his window to enquire what was the problem.

Replied Bill dryly, "There's a cow on the line."

"Where, where?" panicked the signalman.

"Here, this old thing," retorted Bill patting the side of his decidedly steam-shy Derby Class Four!

Fast and furious

More from Mickey. "On one run from Hellifield to Carlisle with the down Thames Clyde

Express we started off twenty minutes down. Our locomotive was in fine fettle rocketing over the section from Ribblehead to Ais Gill where we nearly managed the magical ton. We eventually arrived in Carlisle bang on time.

Another very different type of driver chastised me for blowing off as we left Carlisle travelling south. I retorted that he should get the steam used rather than creeping around the countryside.

On yet another trip I goaded the driver into accepting a bet that we could climb to Ais Gill without stopping for water at Appleby. We had not overmuch left at that point but aimed to top up from the water troughs at Garsdale. It didn't work out like that. Something had been through shortly before us and the troughs had yet to refill. We tottered into Blea Moor loop to replenish supplies.

Stan Maunders was a smashing driver and really nice bloke to work with. I was firing with him on his last trip from Carlisle to Hellifield before retirement and wanted to ensure it was a memorable occasion. I rang Control at Carlisle and explained the situation, requesting that they sidetrack another freight in front which was going down the Lanky, that is the line to Blackburn from Hellifield. Reluctantly they agreed, the earlier freight would go into the lie-by siding at Kirkby Stephen.

We set off with our 'Crab', a 2-6-0 Mogul locomotive which was in good nick and ideal for fast freight. I had both injectors on and coal was being sucked off the shovel, it was pulling that well. Through Blea Moor Tunnel we had fire at both ends, so much was going through the chimney. We had to stop at Blea Moor to take on more water. Stan reckoned it the best trip he had made over the Drag and a fitting finale to his career."

Gordon Hodgson

Gordon is a regular steam driver and sometime fireman over the Settle-Carlisle on the charter specials using the line. I have come to know him through stewarding on some of them. You are invariably granted an exciting and memorable run with him at the helm which is what the paying passengers savour. Here is a little about his early railway career.

"I was eighteen when I started on the railway as, living in the country, transport was required to get into Carlisle from my home some eighteen miles out. Passing my driving test, a 1935 Austin Ruby allowed me to follow my passion for working on the railway. Canal shed was then still open and, being eighteen I rose quickly through the ranks. After a short spell as cleaner it was firing on local trip working, shunting and the Silloth run often with a J39, a good strong engine, free steaming though a little rough.

I fired for the last two years of steam over the Waverley route. This was luck really, one chap in the link was work shy and another didn't get on with his mate. The foreman was very good at letting me take over for a period of a month or so at a time. There were four LNER A3 types

Time for a fag at Blea Moor as the 'Crab' 2-6-0 takes water.

Gordon Hodgson alongside and in the cab of Royal Scot class 46115 'Scots Guardsman'.

allocated to Canal shed. They were known colloquially as 'Canal Pets' being 60068 'Sir Visto', 79 'Bayardo', 93 'Coronach' (my favourite) and 95 'Flamingo'.

During 1963 Canal shed was closed and all the staff transferred to Kingmoor. Prior to that if Kingmoor was short of a fireman, there was the chance of a run over the S&C. I well remember my first firing turn over Ais Gill, though not the locomotive. It is a hard road but then so too was the Waverley which actually boasted steeper gradients.

In passing, both the Thames-Clyde and Waverley expresses were limited to nine coaches though the sleeper would be a heavier train at night with an easier schedule. Just as well. I've fired with an A3 up front during the summer months when extra coaches plus three or four vans would take the weight way above the 350 tons limit. 480 tons was nearer the mark. At Edinburgh Haymarket shed there were a couple of A2s which were theoretically more powerful though given the chance we would take back our A3 when it had been serviced. The same load was taken forward over the S&C though with a different locomotive.

The Waverley route was a great challenge to any fireman with a ruling grade as steep as 1 in 65. However the S&C beat it into a cocked hat as regards scenery. I was fair bowled over by it. Carlisle to Aisgill is fifty-two miles. With an engine short of steam that is a long way. Stopping for a blow-up was not unusual, there were some heavy trains."

The big switch

"One I am unlikely to forget. It was a Jubilee, possibly 'Alberta', on a freight and in a terrible state. So we struggled all the way to Leeds with this 5X. We put it on shed at Holbeck and went off for a meal and rest. In the evening we returned, looked at the engine board and we were booked for the same loco back. There was another freight due to follow us half an hour later to Carlisle with a Holbeck crew. This was booked with a brand new Kingmoor Black Five. My mate rummaged around in his pocket, finally producing a piece of chalk. I was instructed to keep obbo while he rubbed out the two numbers and switched them round. At the booking office my mate remarked,

'Kept a good un for us then?'

'Oh aye, allus keep a good un for you Carlisle lads.'

We nipped off sharpish with the new engine down to Stourton to pick up our train before, passing Holbeck once more, the crew on our former loco were spied shouting and waving fists at us!"

Diesel days

"Promotion more or less came to a halt with the advent of the diesel. Many lads took the money and were paid off. I think I was offered the majestic sum of £350. There was still an element of steam as early diesels had steam heating. Other than that, much of the time we were able to try our hands at the controls, learning the road.

Several of the older drivers struggled with the early diesels, many being in awe of them. Sometimes there was the choice of either steam or diesel locomotive. I would entreat the driver, 'Take the steam, take the steamer.' I usually got told where to go. I was mad on steam.

On a diesel, every ten minutes the second man was required to go back into the engine compartment and make a note of the readings of oil pressure, water pressure, etcetera. There were seven of them. A particularly nervous driver had made out little bits of paper with all these dials drawn on, so that the second man had to fill in the pointer on each dial.

Well, I got mighty fed up with this so started filling in ficticious readings. The engine would shut down at 12psi water pressure, maximum water temperature was 210 Fahrenheit and many more. So I would show the water pressure at 14, water temperature at 212 and so on. I showed this to the driver who hit the roof, 'It's going to stop, going to stop, going to blow up.' Happy days!"

Near disaster

Gary Richards based at Blackburn remembers being secondman on a freight train bound for Carlisle New Yard. This would be between 1968 and 1972.

"Approaching Howe & Co's signal box, I looked back down the train and was amazed to see that a wagon axlebox was ablaze. It was in fact glowing yellow with heat. Most unusual as all vehicles by this time were fitted with roller-bearing boxes.

My driver stopped the train at the signal box where it was decided to leave the wagon, a 16-ton box van, in the sidings. Looking at the label we saw that it was carrying army munitions. The guard notified district Control who, I believe, liaised with Carlisle Fire Service. The train crew extinguished the fire, fortunately leaving the box van some distance from the signal box.

On our return journey some three hours later we saw that the fire appeared to be out. Several hours later the van exploded. It was completely destroyed, the only recognisable components being the four wheels. Had the van been left near the signal box, it would without doubt have resulted in serious injury to the signalman on duty. For a couple of days after, squads of soldiers scoured the locality looking for the munitions which had been scattered over a large area.

As might be imagined there was quite an inquiry following this incident with awkward questions being asked of several parties."

Second men should be good sprinters

Another incident from Gary which might well have had a more serious outcome:

"Round about 1966 I was second man on a Carlisle Banbury freight. We were routed into the up goods loop at Hellifield where we learnt that a Class 40 diesel that had failed was waiting in the down loop to be collected for recovery to Crewe Works. We were assigned to do just this.

Taking his camera with him on the footplate, Gordon Hodgson has been in a position to capture scenes denied to the average photographer.

Above: An amazing shot taken when climbing Mallerstang towards Ais Gill summit. The camera is looking back from the cab of 777 'Sir Lamiel' across the tender to the train engine Black Five 5407.

Far away from crowds of enthusiasts, Midland Compound 1000 and Jubilee 5690 'Leander' await their train at Howe & Co's Siding in the Eden Valley. The reason for this unique situation was that the chimney of the Compound was deemed to be too close to the overhead wires at Carlisle. A diesel therefore brought the train south to this point on February 12th, 1983.

Views from the footplate of 'Leander' as it approaches the south portal of Blea Moor tunnel (above) and crosses Arten Gill viaduct. (below).

Now there was a peculiarity about the Class 40 with regard to the handbrakes which were not sufficiently strong to hold them on a gradient. That being so they were provided with scotches in each cab to place beneath the leading wheels at either end.

We were aware of this and having uncoupled from our train crossed to the down loop to collect the Class 40 approaching it at very low speed. However the slightest nudge set it rolling, pushing the scotches aside. The signalman in Hellifield North box was alive to this and, rather than derail the locomotive at the trap points at the end of the loop, opened them to let it out onto the main line. We followed and gradually caught up with the runaway which was only travelling slowly. I arranged with my driver that when we got close enough I would jump down, run alongside and try to open the door of the escapee. Easier said than done, it started to gain on me. Deciding that discretion was the better part of valour I let it go, my driver and locomotive following at a distance.

The Hellifield signalman had in the meantime sent bell code 4.5.5 to his colleague at Settle Junction, train running away on the right line, doubtless clarifying this by internal phone. The signalman there as a result routed both locomotives onto the Carnforth branch which although initially level soon starts to climb Giggleswick bank. Here the runaway's antics came to an end, it being safely secured to our Class 40. I was picked up on the way back to Hellifield.

I don't think that sort of thing would be allowed these days. By the way, that problem with the Class 40 was never to my knowledge satisfactorily resolved."

Footplate jollies

When he was preparing a book on the Settle-Carlisle back in the 1960s, Bill Mitchell managed to arrange a footplate pass on trip 85, the Horton in Ribblesdale to Appleby shunt hauled by locomotive No 75011. Bill Dakin accompanied by fireman Eddie (Ted) Robson were the crew.

A memorable though hardly good start was made when the train neglected to stop at Settle as arranged to pick up Bill and the traction inspector accompanying him. The crew did however wave. Very shortly there was a telephone call from Horton in Ribblesdale station, the crew apologising for the confusion and advising they would return to Settle. George Horner was the signalman on duty at Horton and he arranged for the engine to shunt its wagons into the down quarry siding prior to popping down to Settle to pick up Bill and the inspector.

Back at Horton, Bill Dakin departed to have a 'crack' with George in the signal box while Bill Mitchell photographed his fireman sat at the controls. Blea Moor, Garsdale water troughs and Kirkby Stephen were also recorded. In fact there was considerable discussion as to whether they should reach Kirkby Stephen, the inspector mentioning a mess coach which needed collecting there and returning to Ais Gill in preparation for Sunday ballast work.

Driver Dakin was not convinced that they had time to get to Kirkby and back as he had promised his wife that he would be home early that day. At that moment the day's workings on the S&C depended on the drivers matrimonial relationship!

The mess coach was collected and later stabled at Ais Gill on the return leg in preparation for Sunday work.

Bill Mitchell's numerous books on the railway have become compulsive reading for devotees of the line.

Watering

A tale is told of the crew of a northbound freight stopping at Appleby to take water. There is adjacent the platform a public house, The Station, so they slipped in for a quick one while the tender was filled. Seems it was actually a slow one, they on leaving the pub being faced by a torrent of water descending the steep hill into town.

More recently at Appleby, I was stewarding on a steam charter which as usual stopped there going south to take water at the refurbished water crane sponsored by Appleby Round Table. The support crew having finished this exercise was seen to form a circle by the cab of I believe No.6201 'Princess Elizabeth'. There was a period of silence before the ashes of one of their number were tossed into the firebox as the train pulled away.

Not too many people are cremated twice.

Trouble with shifts

Back to Mickey Venn who used to ride a motorbike to get on shift. Often it would break down and he would more than once call on Derek Soames at Settle to stop an up train to give him a lift to Skipton. Another time when Derek was not on duty he got a call through to Control requesting permission to stop an up parcels train for a lift. Control said, "No", so I told them, "It won't be going beyond Skipton."

Came the retort, "Why?"

"Because I'm firing it to Leeds."

The train was stopped.

"When I was but a cleaner I was a cheeky beggar knowing it all. Just once, driver Teddy Hudson, a lovely man, lost patience with me, pouring a full billy of tea over my head, as a result having to drive all the way to Carlisle tealess!

I was on my motorbike riding from Settle to Hellifield on shift when I was held up by council workmen the far side of Long Preston. They had single-line traffic controlled by lights and deliberately held me up an inordinate time. When I eventually got a green, I stuck out a leg as I roared past kicking over every one of their bollards. I wasn't held up again.

On another occasion early one dark morning when my bike refused to start, I stood in Settle Market Place trying without success to thumb a lift to get me to Hellifield. Eventually getting desperate, I stood in the middle of the road defying an eight-wheeled quarry lorry to run me

75014 and 70000 'Britannia' at Appleby on a southbound special. Many steam charters pause here to use the refurbished water crane sponsored by Appleby Round Table.

down. The driver stopped, wound down his window and gave me a load of abuse. Meantime I had spotted something. 'Never mind then,' I told him, 'You won't be going far.'

'How's that then?'

'Because you have the tipper in the up position.' Clearly it had been left like this overnight to drain and he had forgotten it. 'Get to the narrow arch at the east of Settle below the railway, it will hit it and catapult you through the windscreen.'

I got my lift."

Get your teeth into the job

Albert Lawson, a Hellifield driver, was cycling through Long Preston one snowy day to go on shift. Climbing the bank at the far side, he had a sneezing fit shooting out his false teeth into a deep drift. Try as he might he could not find them. Two months later he was about to cough up the price of a new pair when a council workman aware of his plight came across and returned them.

Mickey late again

"One winter's day at Skipton that bike failed again so I tried to cadge a lift on a goods train, asking the driver to slow at Giggleswick bank to let me drop off. He was having none of it. The guard took pity on me inviting me on board. As we approached the bank he, the guard, screwed down his brake in the van and the train almost came to a halt allowing me to jump off in safety.

Returning from late duty at Hellifield on my motorbike and passing through Settle a police motor patrol spotted that I had no rear light. I knew this as the front light was over powerful. Anyway, by the time they had turned round I had a fair start. Instead of heading straight home – they knew where I lived – I headed through town and abandoned my bike in a hedgerow before walking home. I told Mum what had happened and to tell the police when they called that I was not at home. They arrived and departed while I slept soundly upstairs."

In the spirit of helpfulness

"Once a friend living at Ingfield close to the railway at Settle asked me to drop off some coal as we passed his house at the lineside. I shoved off a massive slab which didn't break, smashing its way through the side of his garage. He never asked again."

The long wait

At Low House Crossing north-west of Armathwaite a freight train was stopped for an inordinate time, so long in fact that having assertained from the signalman that they would be there for hours rather than minutes, the fireman was despatched to seek sustenance. Down in the village he approached the local inn for guidance. This was gladly given provided that he, the fireman, made up a four at dominoes. The driver's lunch was further delayed, though when it eventually arrived the meat pies, warmed up on a shovel back. tasted just grand.

Squeaky clean

Did you know that the Settle-Carlisle was for a brief period without doubt the cleanest line in the country? This was at the time that Selside signal box was still open – 30 October 1968 at around 00.15.

A Type 4 2000 horse power diesel No 305 was hauling the Preston to Carlisle freight consisting of forty-seven vehicles on a busy yet wild night when the two-man crew both dozed off, passing the signals at Horton and the Selside distant before ramming the rear of a stationary goods held at Selside. Our old friend George Horner was on duty at Selside when he received bell 4.5.5 from Horton, train running away on right line. He had stopped a similar goods from Warrington to Carlisle at his starter signal due to the failure of another locomotive and train on the northbound line in the area of Blea Moor. The second train of forty-seven vehicles ploughed into the rear of the first causing the derailment of thirty-nine wagons plus the second locomotive.

Many of the vans derailed in the first train contained packets of Persil and large drums of caustic soda flake. These were spread over a wide area, doubtless some packets of soap powder finding local use.

Fortunately the only injury was to the guard of the first train held at Selside, who managed to get clear before the impact though in the darkness blundered into some spilt caustic soda ruining his uniform and sustaining minor burns to a leg. A contributory factor to the accident was possibly the cab ventilation, the roof vents having been stuffed up with newspaper, seemingly a regular occurrence on this type of locomotive.

Rage!

Mickey Venn: "Driver Teddy Earnshaw was normally a very steady fellow to work with. Not over large but strong and a devil when roused. I was firing for him when we were put inside at Appleby so we went off to the mess cabin at the end of the up platform. Well, you have never seen such a tip. It was filthy, mice running around, muck and piles of debris everywhere. Teddy went berserk, Jesus upsetting the moneylenders' table in the temple had nothing on him. I just watched spellbound until the recent inmates fled. We cleaned the place out and had a decent brew."

Mickey Venn put on this spectacular pre-arranged smoke display for the photographer. He was firing Royal Scot class 46115 'Scots Guardsman' at Baron Wood, near Armathwaite.

Steam revival

During 1978 steam returned to the Settle-Carlisle with a regular weekend charter train over the Drag. "I got my ticket to drive in 1980." So recounts Gordon Hodgson:

"4771 'Green Arrow' was the first steamer to cross Ais Gill and is a great engine. Not for nothing were the V2s known as the engines that won the war, their pulling power being legendary. In those early years two of my favourites were the Black Fives – 5407, Paddy Smith's engine and 5305, both highly reliable.

In fact preserved locomotives receive much greater care now than they ever did during their former lives. Don't forget some are pushing ninety years old. On the down side, with rare exceptions such as the Appleby water tower and crane, there are not the facilities available that once were taken as commonplace. Turntables and watertroughs are classic examples. When something goes wrong it is very much up to the driver, fireman and the invaluable support crew riding next to the engine in their own coach to sort things out.

One of those early trips was with 'Flying Scotsman' travelling north. I was firing, I forget who was driving, Ronnie Gerrard was the inspector. We stopped three times for a blow up. The owner's representative was on board and criticising my firing. Ronnie turned round and told him, 'Look, if it won't steam for Gordon, it won't steam for anybody else.' Anyway he persisted and eventually was handed the shovel – with a conspicuous lack of success. 'Scotsman' was stopped when we got to Carlisle.

Another difficult day was with a Western Region King No 6024 'King Edward 1'. Again we stopped three times, a problem with the smokebox door I believe, it just would not seal. I was doing the inspector's job that day. It would go really well for forty miles and then the draughting caused the fire to start to lift and much would go straight up the blastpipe. It was set up for different coal which didn't help. The smokebox filled up and that was that. Most embarrassing. It was a pity as it is a beautiful engine and well maintained."

The trouble with water

"'Green Arrow' pulled above its weight, an excellent rider and steamed well provided you had enough water! We had taken over at Blackburn where the engine was watered. We should have taken more at Garsdale but crews were not keen on this, the water coming off the fells and being very acidic. So we headed for Appleby and just made it. I told the crew it was cutting things too fine, so next time Garsdale, after all the tender is only a standard 4,000 gallons.

Next time it was Preston to Garsdale for water though not much steam is needed up to Blackburn. Paul Kane was fireman and driver Brian Greenson. Paul isn't easily discouraged but 4771 was struggling up the bank towards Hellifield and pressure had dropped to 150 pounds. The fire wasn't drawing so I thought the spark arrester might have got clogged up. At Hellifield we opened the smokebox door – very little problem there.

So we struggled on manfully, eventually reaching Blea Moor tunnel. We had half an inch of water in the boiler and 150 pounds of steam. Just into the tunnel and the injector blew off. Normally there is no trouble with these on 'Green Arrow'. I tried to put it on again. Again it blew off. The penny dropped, we were virtually running on empty. There was only one thing to do, get out of the tunnel which of course levels off in the middle. We eventually drifted to a halt over Arten Gill Viaduct.

Panic! 'What do we do now?' ask the crew. I tell them to drop the fire and I will break the good news to Control. Ray Towell from the NRM was on board, 'Can't we go light engine to Dent and get the fire brigade?' What up that hill and round those bends?

Well I couldn't get a signal on the phone so started to climb the fellside more in hope than expectation just as one of the support crew arrived with the news that there is a stream running off the fellside a hundred yards back. So we go and have a look at it. The stream is culverted and higher than the tender so we back up the train, climb out with some fire hose, put it in the stream and dam it up behind. Well, we watched the water force its way up the hose – acid and all – and into the tender. After a couple of minutes I tried the injector again – praise be – it worked. That injector singing was one of the sweetest sounds I ever heard.

There was a postscript to the 'Green Arrow' saga. About a week later I received a parcel through the post. Inside was one of those cardboard tubes that usually contain a bottle of malt. What a kind thought. The hard stuff in this one was however acidic water as revealed by the label which read, 'Arten Gill Water. Refreshes engines other waters cannot reach!' I never did find out who sent it."

Light relief

"At Settle station in one of the trefoils in the up platform is an effigy of Mickey Mouse. When I first started firing over the line, it was nailed to a telegraph pole at Dent station. The tale is that a platelayer had found him and nailed him up there to mark the height of the snow in 1947. We firemen used to throw lumps of coal trying to hit it. The signalman appreciated the coal, it being useful for his fire.

When Dent box was wantonly destroyed, it was simply a matter of chucking in half a gallon of paraffin and putting a match to it. The telegraph pole went up too and we were quite sad at losing Mickey. A few months later he reappeared at Settle. Someone obviously took pity on him. Later still, to keep him company [in the next opening], Minnie Mouse appeared. There is just one space left now."

Wash and brush-up

"Back to water and one of the worst experiences was when we used to get it from the Express Dairy at Appleby before the water tower and column were erected. 'Sir Nigel Gresley' was the

The early diesels were often unreliable and more than one locomotive could be needed to complete a journey. This scene at Blea Moor, with a train triple-headed by a pair of class 20s and a 47, is a reminder of those days.

engine which was uncoupled from the train and ran the few hundred yards to the dairy. They must have been cleaning their tanks. We ended up with a tenderful of detergent. Talk about priming. The Gresley engines had this tendency. When you blew the whistle bubbles came out either side. What a trip we had that day. When they got it back to York they had to wash out the boiler half a dozen times. Folk think water is just water but it isn't, there is a deal more to it than that.

Happily the problems that occurred twenty-five to thirty years back have taught steam crews a great deal. This is not to say problems do not occur, simply that usually the support crews can handle them, we hope!"

As my memory serves, Gordon was fireman on a southbound run fromCarlisle to Hellifield, over fifty miles from near sea level to the summit of Ais Gill at 1,169 feet. The locomotive was the Britannia, 'Oliver Cromwell'. When we reached Hellifield I walked down to the engine to congratulate the crew on an excellent run. Gordon, by then seventy or near enough, had barely broken sweat.

This class 31 diesel hauling the daily ballast train from Ribblehead caught fire near Settle one day in January 1986. The guard had a camera and was able to record the incident.

Fire – and 'Gresley' to the rescue

Shortly before the daily ballast train ceased to run from the quarry at Ribblehead in January 1986, one of the last workings was proceeding steadily south towards Settle Junction. It was hauled by a class 31 diesel which in the area of Settle suffered a fire in the engine compartment. The driver brought it safely to a halt by the bridge adjacent the former toll house on the original road leading into and a mile east of Settle. Contact was made with the local fire brigade who attended. One member of this was David Richardson, who recalls them getting a hose down to the track and into the engine compartment to spray everything to cool and make the locomotive safe. David is one of the team who later carried out a deal of work moving and restoring Settle

An even more remarkable incident befell the ballast train when its class 47 diesel locomotive failed north of Settle Junction. This was not unusual, though the rescue operation may well have been unique. The low-powered class 25 sent to its rescue proved unable to haul the train up the grade to Hellifield. A4 'Sir Nigel Gresley' happened to be travelling tender-first from Carnforth and was successfully commandeered to assist in the rescue.

Station signal box. Eventually a relief locomotive was located and sent to rescue the ballast train.

It was according to Derek Soames not unusual for diesels of that time to fail, particularly on this duty. He was on duty one day when a class 47 on the ballast train failed north of Settle Junction. Derek was notified and a Class 25 located and sent to rescue the train. This was fine going down the grade to Settle Junction. He however realised that this low-powered diesel was unlikely to pull around 130 tons of dead locomotive plus its train of loaded hoppers up the grade to Hellifield let alone any further. Settle Junction is the low point at the southern end of the S&C at 450 feet. Hellifield is at 500 feet and Settle Station 510 feet.

Help was however at hand in the unlikely form of 'Sir Nigel Gresley' proceeding tender-first from Carnforth to take over the northbound leg of the Cumbrian Mountain Express. Derek brought it to a halt at the signal guarding Settle Junction and advised the crew of the problem. "Might they assist in moving the train to Hellifield?" They were happy to oblige resulting in the unique situation of 'Gresley' heading this entourage tender-first followed by the Class 25 also supplying traction, then the Class 47 with its train of ballast. The guard took a photograph of the fire on the Class 31 and a solitary bystander of the very mixed freight, from both of whom Derek obtained copies. Express lamps were being displayed on 'Gresley'. As Derek later remarked, "Well it was going express through Long Preston."

The sequel was when the signalmen's inspector challenged him over his actions. "Well," retorted Derek, "there was a problem and it wanted sorting, all done within half an hour."

"That's alright," came the reply, "but what would have happened if 'Gresley' had been damaged, you should have contacted Control."

"Yes," came back Derek, "and the whole shooting match would have been held up for hours." Nothing more was heard of the incident.

Crew training

During 1993 a series of crew training days were held over three weeks for Railtrack staff wishing to learn the art of driving and firing steam locomotives. The initiative for this came from David Ward, Head of Special Trains at Intercity. Initially the concept was to recruit and train twelve new steam drivers and firemen from the ranks of diesel and electric loco drivers based in Carlisle. A Class Four 2-6-4 tank locomotive No. 80080 (described by a crew member as "eight nothing nothing eight nothing"), on loan from the Midland Railway Centre at Butterley in Derbyshire, hauled four coaches between Carlisle and Kirkby Stephen twice a day over those three weeks.

The public might for a modest charge – £10 – ride on them. This action, an afterthought, raised some useful revenue. Needless to say Bill Mitchell and I spent some time on this train.

Gordon Hodgson on these crew training trips: "After a time the York drivers in particular were retiring. So the decision was made to train some new firemen while existing ones moved up to driving. In those days it was possible to run round the train at Kirkby Stephen. A good pal of

Driver Gordon Hodgson has taken time off the footplate to photograph steam specials.
Above: 9F 99220 'Evening Star' threads Baron's Wood in the Eden Valley.
Below: Standard Class 4 76029 and West Country class 34067 'Tangmere' hauling the Pines Express through Kirkby Stephen.

Class 4 80080 arrives at Kirkby Stephen station on a crew training run in 1993.

mine – and a conscientious railwayman – was to take his driving passing-out exam next day under the watchful eye of Chief Inspector Bill Andrew. Bearing in mind the water tanks were on the side of the locomotive, he had made a clear chalk mark where the steps off the footplate should match up to the Appleby water column, leaving the filler tank opening in exactly the right position. What a good idea.

Now my pal had one problem, he was accident-prone. If anything was going to happen, it happened to him. It did. During the night there was a fall of snow obscuring the mark, so it was back to guesswork."

An ex-driver riding on the Kirkby-Carlisle shuttle recounted tales from years back: "You would enter this marshalling yard where a shunter there was known as Picasso. Why, while instructing you where he wanted wagons shunted, he would say, 'Now let me put you in the picture?'"

Again the same driver describing the Class Four tank: "Aye, these were known as bacon slicers, cos the reversing gear was unusually in the shape of a large vertical wheel of just about the same dimensions."

Non Stop

And finally driver Kenny Earnshaw who was nicknamed 'Non Stop' as he regularly forgot to stop at stations when on passenger trains. In other respects he was by all accounts a smashing man.

Passengers might beg to differ.

Chapter Six

Snow - the Curse of the Settle Carlisle

Back to back with Mickey Venn

"Shale cutting near Dent was blocked by snow. Two Class Four locomotives tender to tender with a plough each end were sent up to clear it. We rushed it at seventy mph but the second driver got cold feet and eased off. Kenny Earnshaw was my driver and went back to remonstrate with the second crew. The trouble was much of the snow our plough threw up landed on their tender and cab travelling as they were in reverse. We tried again with similar results. At the third attempt we did eventually get through. We were out that day for eighteen hours. In the lead engine, snow would force its way in through every gap, that coming from below being like white sausage."

Mountainous drifts of snow block Shale cutting, near Dent, in the winter of 1947.

Ais Gill in 1978 with only one line of rails clear and a diesel locomotive still stranded.

Single-line working

Another incident he recalled concerned snow duty when they broke through on the down line from Ais Gill to Kirkby Stephen:

"We set off back on the same line, it being the only one open, the signalman at Kirkby supposedly having advised Ais Gill. An express was however entering that same section on that line, a catastrophe only being avoided when the signalman at the summit waggled his signals to draw attention to the situation. Fortunately the guard of this train was alert, taking action by applying the emergency brake in his van thus bringing the train to a halt. My driver mounted the steps at Kirkby Stephen three at a time intent on telling the signalman what he intended to do to him."

Decades earlier, Harold Harper of Garsdale was cutting into a snowdrift at Ais Gill with a shovel when, as was the practice at the time, a southbound express stopped to uncouple its pilot engine at the end of the long climb from Carlisle. An inquisitive passenger hanging out from a window shouted, "My dad says that if you have a job on the railway you have bread and butter for life – you haven't got much jam though."

The snowplough train crosses to the down roads at Blea Moor, posing for the photographer.

Inspector from afar

On a less serious note George Horner remembers a new signalmen's inspector making his first visit to Blea Moor on a grand bright summer's day.

"See for miles," says he. "What a grand spot to work."

"Aye, can be," retorts George. "Bit different when the snowflakes is flying about."

"Same as any other ruddy railway, you folk up here don't think there is any other railway".

"Aye, alreet."

George held his peace for over three years until when next he met the inspector. It was a wild winter's day, the inspector being on snowplough duty, a position George had filled back in the rare winter of '63. Now he had moved down the line to the box at Horton in Ribblesdale.

The snowplough train fought its way up to Ribblehead, crossed to the up road, landing back at Horton some time later. The inspector dismounted and with difficulty made his way to the signal box.

George remembers he were a whiskery sort of fella and every whisker bore an icicle. He came in looking like the abominable snowman with:

"I've nivver been in such a spot in all mi life."

"Same as any other ruddy railway."

"Shut thi gob, I know what I said."

George used to laugh like a drain about this one.

At Salt Lake Cottages a quarter mile short of Ribblehead station, back in 1947, the inhabitants – railway workers – built a basic platform out of snow. Sometimes like Nancy they rode down and back to Settle on a snowplough train. Barter took place on this platform, coal being exchanged for home-reared bacon.

Blizzard conditions

Cecil (Sandy) Sanderson, stationmaster at Dent, is unlikely to forget the night his son was born at Dent Station House during the winter of 1941-2. "A blizzard was raging. I had managed to get a nurse up to Dent but a doctor was required. Meantime I was on single line working due to the drifts building up between Kirkby Stephen and Ribblehead. Even the ploughs were getting stuck. Control allowed an express from Carlisle the road." Sandy was not amused, desperately wanting to get back to his wife at Dent.

He arranged for the ploughs to run ahead of the express which thankfully had only four carriages. When it arrived at Kirkby Stephen, he was amazed to find the driver to be an old friend who promised to get him through. Drifts had already built up behind the plough going up Mallerstang. The driver put all on until the loco began to slip. He backed up and had another go being mindful of the catch points which Sandy warned him about. Eventually they did make Dent and miraculously so did the doctor – from Hawes.

During the same period Sandy was again on snow duty when a massive drift built up near the north portal of Blea Moor Tunnel. The plough train with Sandy on board charged around the fellside from Dent station to Arten Gill and Dent Head. Near Arten Gill there was a resounding crash as a telegraph pole fell across their path. Keeping power on and, despite the thought that they might be off the road, they blasted through the drift and into the tunnel.

There was another tremendous crash inside the tunnel, and glass flew all over the shop. The train was stopped, Sandy walked back to locate the remains of a monstrous icicle that had formed in one of the air shafts and was as thick as his body. The line was blocked until several more were cleared.

Deep midwinter at Dent – a notorious location for drifting snow.

Dent Head viaduct can look wonderful in winter, but this stretch of line was more frightening than picturesque during snow-clearing operations in the winter of 1941-42.

This photograph of snow-clearing at Dent in 1947 struck a special chord with one member of the audience at an audio-visual show. She recognised her husband, then Corporal Alker, at far right. The result was an interview with Donald Alker – and some fascinating memories of the diabolical conditions on that day.

A memory from 1947

One winter's evening I was presenting my first audio-visual show on the Settle-Carlisle, 'Against the Grade', at Hornby in the Lune Valley. Just prior to the interval I showed some slides taken (with permission) from prints of the massive drifts around Dent and Garsdale in 1947. Suddenly there was a cry from the audience. During the interval a lady came round to say that on one such slide her husband in his army uniform was on snow-clearing duties.

As a result I arranged to meet and interview Donald Alker at his home in the village. This is his tale:

"During 1947 I was billeted with other members of the East Lancs Regiment at Preston. In the middle of a bitterly cold February night we were awoken by the Sergeant Major with a big stick banging on the wooden walled billets, followed by the orderly sergeant. Instructed to get up at once, put on as much warm underwear as possible and full battledress, we were formed up in threes and marched to Preston station. Haversack rations were issued, then we boarded a rake of icy cold none corridor carriages. Lighting was at a premium, the war being nobbut over.

After many stops and starts we drifted into the back of beyond, I'm still not sure where it was though there were steep-eaved cottages close to the platform with snow right up the walls and to the eaves of the end one.

Hot tea was provided plus shovels before we re-boarded the train for our worksite. Our instructions were to dig out the railway as far as the tunnel. Which tunnel you may well ask? God it was hard. I was nineteen years old then and a PTI. The snow was loaded on low-sided wagons which a locomotive then drew away to a viaduct where it was tipped over the side.

By 4pm our work was finished. Two stripes carried some clout enabling me to cadge a lift back on a locomotive. I took off my greatcoat which then stood up solid in the tender, I thought it was someone behind me."

The steep-eaved cottages were of course Garsdale, their work site beyond being the water troughs leading to Rise Hill Tunnel. The viaduct was Dandry Mire.

Some Italian POWs were used on snow-clearing duties with mixed results, some detraining at one door, being issued with shovels, chucking these over a bridge and climbing back into the carriage at the other end. Shovels were found years after below this bridge.

Corporal Alker, who in true military fashion was woken in the middle of the night to go from Preston to Garsdale in full battledress. Along with other members of the East Lancs Regiment, his instructions were to dig out the line as far as Rise Hill Tunnel.

The Sergeant Major knocks up all the huts.

Good colour photos of railways from the mid-1940s are rare – and those of the upper reaches of the Settle-Carlisle virtually non-existent. This remarkable image captures members of the East Lancs Regiment obeying orders to dig out Garsdale water troughs during their memorable 1947 visit.

These railway cottages at Garsdale had snow right up the walls in 1947 and were understandably seen by Donald Alker as 'the back of beyond'.

Winters can still be bleak at Blea Moor, as shown in this view of a rake of class 156 Sprinters heading north.

Rough times in the lowlands

It wasn't just on the notorious high stretch of railway between Kirkby Stephen and Ribblehead that drifts occurred. Alan Dugdale was at Griseburn box between Kirkby Stephen and Appleby in 1947, and here is his story:

"I was lodging at Asby in 1947, three miles from the box. I had a smashing landlady and she warned me on this particular day that if I got to work, I should never get back. Well I was on the two to ten shift so I had plenty of time to get there. It took me all morning.

I looked out at 10pm and the cutting in which the box was located was completely snowed in. So I closed my box, told the boxes either side and sat down to wait for relief. There was a mountain of coal, plenty of water and my landlady who obviously knew what she was about had provided tons of grub. In fact you got better food there than I did at home, pigs being regularly killed.

Well, I sat there for three days and three nights before they broke through and what bugged me was that Laurie Heslop and Billy Oliver on the relief shifts got paid just the same as me. And I had sat there for three days and three nights!"

A new inspector

During February 1963 Derek Soames was signalman at Hellifield North box and remembers how a new locomotive inspector from a more temperate division had just been appointed to Hellifield shed. He was over full of himself and when the plough train was called out instructed the crews to wait for him to accompany them. He was not dressed for the job and certainly had no idea what was involved. Climbing aboard the second engine - the one running tender first - the crew told him where to stand and to hold on tight. Of course the first drift they hit, the snow from the plough came right over the top of the first loco landing on the rudimentary tarpaulin stretched across the rear of the tender and secured to the top of the second locomotive cab.

Needless to say he was soaked to the skin. Sadly his comments have not been recorded for posterity.

Toby Woodhouse, senior signalling technician, and his assistant Dave Mount, set out to trace the cause of lost communication between signal boxes. This was after a period of snow and a thaw had set in. In the cutting above Selside they found half a dozen telegraph poles already down and, as they watched several trees literally marched down the cutting side on a landslip. It was several days before the land was stabilised and normal service resumed. It is worth recording that after he retired, Toby became instrumental in fitting out the newly refurbished Settle Station Signal Box, now a visitor attraction.

Modern times

More recently Malcolm Sissons was a senior engineering technician who covered part of the Settle-Carlisle for seven years from 1995:

"One wild January day my mate and I were called out to Blea Moor. I had learnt from the signalman there that there were two faults. First was the up Blea Moor distant signal at the south end of Blea Moor tunnel. I decided that this was priority so my mate and I having taken a train to Ribblehead set off from there to walk across the viaduct towards the signal box.

Snow was coming down like no one's business, stinging your face something cruel. It was so bad that over the quarter mile length of the viaduct we crawled on our hands and knees. We managed to get across then ran to the box where two mugs of piping hot tea awaited us.

Refreshed, we set off for the signal which was stuck in the off, clear position, whereas the lever in the box was at the on. There is a retaining wall by the signal from which water cascading off drifted onto the signal arm, freezing it at the clear.

So we set to with hammers and cold chisels until eventually its own weight dropped it back to the horizontal, on, position.

Back to the box for another mug of tea apiece, meantime advising the signalman to try the peg [signal] and keep waggling it to avoid a repetition.

'Now, what's your next problem?'

'It's the ground frame into the quarry siding back at Ribblehead, lever 26 won't shift it.'

So off we go back over the viaduct on hands and knees to the relay box at the entrance to the sidings. The whole thing is covered in ice. When we get it open, everything inside is covered in fine snow. So we set to replacing all the relays and fuses, finally contacting the signalman to make sure all is now OK.

'Yes, thanks very much, coming back for another cup of tea?'

'Not ruddy likely, we are on the next train back to civilisation.'"

The down distant signal at Blea Moor has been replaced with a colour light, the signal arm in question being in working order outside the preserved box at Settle where Malcolm is the genius behind many of the items of refurbishment.

Strange how things work out. Malcolm Sissons was Toby Woodhouse's prodigy and, after the latter's passing and the former's retirement, has become resident signal engineer at Settle Station box (acting unpaid!).

Icicle duty

Finally in this chapter the irrepressible Mickey Venn:

"During the bad winter of 1962/3 I was firing a permanent way special on icicle duty inside Blea Moor tunnel. It was a Sunday as we picked up staff and volunteers right up from Hellifield. We stopped at Blea Moor box as instructed to watch the signalman place collars on the levers controlling the down main line behind us. The same should have happened at Dent on the up but someone decided it would suffice to ring them instead.

On these jobs the locomotive would stop beneath a ventilation shaft where its exhaust would melt a deal of the massive icicles, so large they would seriously injure – possibly fatally – train crew hanging out of their cabs.

I was not at all happy with this situation, so took a bag of detonators and set off down the up (Leeds) line placing one at ¼ mile, another at ½ mile before being aware of pressure building up in my ears. A train was entering the tunnel from the northern end! I slammed down three more which would explode as the wheels ran over them before standing back in a refuge as a light engine thundered by. I heard the driver swear at the explosions before making emergency braking. The permanent way staff and volunteers scattered.

The driver understandably kicked up a right fuss and there was an enquiry at Preston. Later when I was in the King Billy in Settle (King William IV Hotel), all the folk from that hair-raising occasion came in and bought me a drink. I recall little else of that day."

Symbolic of the bitter cold in early 2010 was this massive icicle inside one of the Blea Moor tunnel air shafts. In steam days they were melted by a locomotive's exhaust.

January 2010 brought 'proper' winter conditions back to the Settle–Carlisle after an absence of many years. This chilling scene is at Settle station.

Chapter Seven

A Word from the Management

Things that go bump in the night

It was to be the start of a long day for Stan Hall:

"I was on call on 7 April 1964 when the phone rang just after four o'clock in the morning. It was the control office ringing to say that the 8.45pm Class 4 fitted freight from Manchester Ancoats to Carlisle had become derailed near Howe & Co's Sidings signal box, five miles east of Carlisle on the Settle-Carlisle line."

Stanley Hall, Stan to his friends, had taken up his post as Assistant Movements Superintendent at Barrow in Furness Divisonal HQ during October 1963. A career railwayman, his had started on 30 April 1943 as a junior booking clerk at Keighley. That career was to span several decades before he ultimately achieved the position of Head of Signalling and Accidents in the Operations Department at the British Rail Board Headquarters. The words here are by and large as Stan wrote them, extracted from his records of his time at Barrow, particularly regarding the Settle and Carlisle line.

Stan's previous position had been deputy stationmaster at King's Cross, his new parish was rather different covering all the coastal lines from Carnforth round to Carlisle, the West Coast Main Line between the same two points, plus glory of glories the Settle-Carlisle from Settle northwards. He recalls:

Stanley Hall's involvement with the Settle–Carlisle was very different to his previous position as deputy stationmaster at King's Cross. Here he is seen at the London terminus with Harold Macmillan – a prime minister looking up to the crew!

"Control had swung into action to divert trains away from the Midland lines. The Edinburgh sleeper following the freight north had been stopped at Armathwaite where the engine ran round, being diverted to Carlisle via Hellifield where it did another run round before using the Low Gill branch from Clapham to Lowgill (fortunately still available) arriving in Carlisle nearly four hours late. The Glasgow sleeper was similarly dealt with from Appleby.

One of my divisional inspectors gave me a lift from my home at Roose on the outskirts of Barrow to the site – a lovely run along Windermere and over the Kirkstone Pass – and we arrived on site to be confronted by a heap of wreckage. The train consisted of thirty-two vacuum fitted vans and a brakevan hauled by Class 9F 2-10-0 No. 92161, chicken feed for such a powerful locomotive. Sixteen vehicles had been derailed. Five were lying on their sides, two were upside down and one van was in a field. The Kingmoor steam crane arrived on site at 7.27am and it really was an education to see the breakdown gangs at work. The Skipton crane was on its way so that the debris might be tackled from both ends.

The priority in those days was to get on with clearance of the line as quickly as possible so that the permanent way engineer could move in to restore the track and allow the line to be reopened to traffic.

Specialist teams arrived from the permanent way and carriage and wagon department and we set about establishing the cause of the mishap.

A solitary British Transport policeman arrived to keep an eye on the goods traffic spilt from the vans. We welcomed the police presence and regarded them as colleagues. They seemed to spend a deal of time in the mess vans drinking tea but were always there if needed and we always tipped them off if the inspector was on the way.

The mess van was accompanied by a fitter from the loco shed. His culinary expertise extended to keeping the kettle boiling and making sandwiches, whose slices of bread were so thick they might have been used to re-rail wagons. However, if spoken to nicely mess van attendants would fry great platefuls of bacon and eggs and fried bread (white of course), a sumptuous delicacy on a cold, wet morning after a long night's work. The word cholesterol had not been invented in those innocent days and the breakdown crew would have reacted most unfavourably and with suitable invective had they been offered muesli and yoghurt.

When as was often the case, a freight accident occurred out in the country a local farmer might generally be persuaded to part with quantities of ham, eggs and milk, other supplies perhaps being obtained from the village shop. The important thing was to keep the breakdown crews well fed and happy.

Freight accidents were at that time becoming more common despite the speed of such trains having been reduced. In this case the line was cleared by 4.30 the same afternoon, just twelve hours after the derailment. The permanent way people got to work, re-opening the up main line just after midnight and the down main at 3.20am, in time for the 8.45pm freight from Ancoats!

The inquiry was held two days later in Carlisle. The carriage and wagon engineer had identified and examined the first vehicle to become derailed and found that one of the springs was weak with almost an inch less camber than that diagonally opposite. This allowed a wheel to climb the outside rail on the right hand curve past Howe & Co's signal box. Coupled with a very slight track defect prior to the point of derailment and the indication from signal box records that the train was travelling at between 55 and 60 mph, the combination was dynamite. Although the line speed was 70 mph, freight was restricted to 50 mph. In fairness to the crew there was no speedometer on the locomotive and it was a very dark night making it difficult for the driver to accurately assess his speed."

The mystery of the missing motor cars

Stan continues: "A most unusual mishap occurred on 7 December 1964. There was a strong south-westerly gale accompanied by heavy rain which continued into the night. The wind howled round our house in Roose on the outskirts of Barrow as rain lashed the windows. Sleep was punctuated by the sound of breaking glass as our greenhouse was systematically demolished. I was not really surprised to be woken at 4.0am, again by the sound of the telephone. This was way before bedside phones and central heating as I crept downstairs in my dressing gown, shivering by the phone as the Control Office gave me some astounding news.

'You won't believe this,' said the voice of the Deputy Chief Controller at the other end of the line. 'I'm not having you on and its not April 1st, but four or five brand new motor cars are lying upside down on the up line on Ribblehead viaduct. They've blown off the Luton-Bathgate car-carrier.'

I got dressed, made my way with difficulty against the howling gale to the office where I picked up one of the pool cars. I then set off in the pitch dark to drive to Ribblehead along flooded roads littered with tree branches. It was a hair-raising drive and I didn't get to Ribblehead until 7.15am, just as dawn was breaking. I was met by the stationmaster and taken into his kitchen for a cup of tea. I expect his wife offered me breakfast too, but there was work to be done. I wanted to see the accident site for myself but I needn't have rushed. The Skipton steam crane didn't arrive on site until 10.0am as it had to collect some flat wagons on which to load the cars. By this time the wind had abated and the rain had ceased.

The thought did enter our heads of just dumping the cars over the side of the viaduct, but there was no great urgency to clear the line and the Humber Super Snipes weighing around two tons apiece were not that badly damaged. Mornings were a fairly quiet time, trains being diverted via Ingleton and Low Gill. Thank goodness we still had that facility; it closed shortly afterwards. TV crews came along during the morning and there was a photo in one of the newspapers.

The line was cleared by 2.0pm and I had another cup of tea courtesy of the stationmaster's wife, before setting off for Ais Gill. The train had been parked up there waiting for a loading inspector to come along and satisfy himself that all the remaining cars were sufficiently secure.

The wreckage of the Humber Super Snipes blown off a car-carrier crossing Ribblehead viaduct on the stormy night of 7 December 1964.

They were. I expect I had another cup of tea with the signalman. I made a point of never refusing a cup of tea because you never knew where the next one was coming from in such a far flung empire.

We had the formal enquiry three days later, at Skipton. We chose Skipton as it was easier of access for the witnesses. The cars were simply secured by metal chocks under the wheels and suitable changes were recommended. The signalmen from Blea Moor, Dent and Garsdale were also witnesses. Signalman Horner senior at the former had spotted the gaps, telephoned his colleague at Dent who confirmed his suspicions and arranged for the train to be stopped at Garsdale for examination. The signalmen should have been rewarded for their vigilance and quick thinking. I don't recall whether they were. If an up train had run into those cars, the result does not bear thinking about. Signalman Horner said he had never known such a wild night in all his experience.

Imagine the scene that night at Garsdale. The wind howling and the rain lashing down in that bleak inhospitable spot. The signalman kept his signals at danger. When the train arrived, he explained to the driver his suspicions, who sent his secondman to fetch the guard to examine the train. They reported back that there were indeed gaps on the train which were not there when it left Leeds. So where were the cars? The stationmaster at Ribblehead didn't have to walk far before he discovered them. He was a brave man (echoes of the Tay Bridge disaster) to venture onto that viaduct in the pitch dark with a gale threatening to pluck him off and hurl him more than a hundred feet onto the bleak moorland below. You had to be made of stern stuff to be an SM on the wilder parts of the S&C.

On the day of the inquiry we had steak and kidney pudding for lunch in Brown Muff's cafe in the High Street at Skipton. At these inquiries we always had two shorthand typists working in rotation because all the evidence was taken down verbatim and signed by the staff as a true record. This avoided arguments at a later date. By coincidence as Christmas was approaching and to persuade the diners to part with some of their cash to buy presents, models were parading around the restaurant in nighties and underwear. OK for the typists but it quite put us off our steak and kidney pud.

It is interesting to note that had the Clapham - Low Gill via Ingleton line been retained the closure of the S&C would have made much more sense. Almost the first day I arrived at Barrow I was shown a signalling plan for the closure of the S&C between Appleby and Ribblehead, this being the most expensive part of the line to maintain. However when the Low Gill line was allowed to close retention of the S&C became of more importance."

And you get paid as well!

"One of the porters at Garsdale was retiring and it was decided that I should travel across there and present him with his long service certificate. It was a whole day's job of course, but I had decided to head off in that direction the previous evening. Rather than travel by car, I took the train to Penrith, then the bus to Appleby, spending the night at the Tufton Arms Hotel. Next morning, a beautiful sunny day, I caught the train to Garsdale accompanied by the district inspector to visit the porter in his own home. He had just retired after over fifty years service, all of it at Garsdale, so he said. He was over seventy years old and hadn't wanted to retire earlier, nor had he ever wanted to leave Garsdale. He and his wife were perfectly happy there. There's a moral here somewhere. He remembered well both the Hawes Junction (Garsdale) and Ais Gill disasters of 1910 and 1913 respectively and had a host of stories to tell. I wish I had taken along a tape recorder.

He lived in one of the row of cottages at the station and his wife received us with old world courtesy. On the dining table was a white tablecloth laid with best china, home-made cakes and delicacies. We sat and chatted for hours and I was quite touched. For them the visit of the assistant superintendent from headquarters was a major event and I was glad that I had gone to present the old porter's certificate in person, rather than just posting it to his stationmaster. Duty done, I said my good-byes and went forward to Horton in Ribblesdale leaning over the rail of the brakevan at the back of the local pick-up goods and surveying the scenery. And to think I was being paid for doing this! Arriving at Horton, I had a tour of the local quarries, which in those days provided quite a lot of traffic. Perhaps one day soon they will do so again.

Really our headquarters was in the wrong place. Carlisle would have been much more convenient but for commercial and political reasons Barrow found favour."

Back of beyond

"On one occasion I needed to visit two or three places on the S&C so I left home after tea, spending the night in an hotel in Carlisle. Next morning with the sun rising into a clear blue sky, I met one of my inspectors and we travelled in the brakevan of the local pick-up to Appleby, then crossed over to the old North Eastern line and proceeded to Warcop, which was an army depot, then on past Kirkby Stephen to the end of the line at Hartley Quarry. Quarry traffic had ceased and that end of the line was soon lifted, so I was glad to have had the chance to revisit it for the last time. We were back in Appleby in time for the up Waverley, so I decided that I would have a footplate ride to Hellifield on one of the ex LNER Pacifics which had been transferred to Holbeck, being held in high regard as good riders.

When the train ran into Appleby I saw that there were already four people on the footplate of the A3 so decided that I would not be welcome. Instead I remained in the town, visiting the Express Dairies Depot. For many years they had sent several milk tanks to London each day, at one time being attached to the rear of the 4.10pm Glasgow to Leeds, but in recent years they were worked into Carlisle to join the tanks from Aspatria."

Luxury

"Steam enthusiasts will never forgive me for this but travelling on the footplate as a passenger was not one of my favourite activities. You couldn't see anything, it was too noisy to talk, you had to keep jumping out of the way of the fireman, plus you were frozen at one side and scorched at the other. It was also an advantage to be dressed for the job. On the other hand I had some grand trips in the cab of some of the English Electric Type 4s – the D200s.

Sorry fellers, the buffet car was my favourite mode of travel. Settle had the Waverley in both directions, Appleby did even better having the St Pancras to Edinburgh in both directions and the 10.25am Leeds to Glasgow as well. One of life's delights was to travel back on the 4.10pm from Glasgow, having dinner in the dining car after it left Carlisle. The diner was a twelve-wheeler of LMS vintage, a splendid vehicle with a splendid crew, who looked after you well. Imagine sitting in a warm and comfortable train feeding your inner self with a good meal washed down with half a bottle of good wine, while feeding your eyes on the wild surroundings as the train heaved itself up Mallerstang. On a dirty night, with the rain lashing down, the contrast between the outside world and the warm, comfortable coach with its contented and well-fed passengers was enormous. On a lovely summer's evening with the setting sun highlighting the tops of the Pennines in all their rich colours it was truly a delight."

Competition time

"One of the more arcane customs of the railway was the best-kept station competition, all the stations in the divisions being obliged to enter. There was also the station garden competition, though this was voluntary. For judging purposes all eighty stations in the division had to be visited. We borrowed the civil engineer's inspection saloon for this purpose. This could either be towed or propelled. In the latter case this involved someone sitting right at the front with communication to the driver in either his steam or diesel cab and sounding the horn as necessary. This was a fought-over responsibility.

It was hard tiring work taking three days to complete but the views were superb. We could have sold tickets for £50 a time. The saloon was equipped with a central kitchen and a steward. We put ourselves away in a siding somewhere for a hot lunch, making sure the train crew had their share.

Day three took us to the S&C, starting off at Settle. The stationmaster, Mr Taylor, was a gardening expert and won the competition every year. He told us that he had planted out 6,000

The engineer's saloon at Ais Gill.

The engineer's inspection saloon at Shotlock Hill tunnel, north of Garsdale. Boasting a central kitchen and a steward, it was regularly borrowed for judging the best-kept station competition.

bedding plants and I could well believe it as I surveyed the platforms. It was a long day but we were well fed and watered, with a noggin or two on the way home when the day's work was over. I kept pinching myself to make sure that I wasn't dreaming it all. Now you can appreciate the reference to being paid to do this.

The awards took place later in the year at the Pheasant Inn, Bassenthwaite, where all the stationmasters and other local officials assembled. The Cockermouth, Keswick and Penrith line was still open then. No doubt it was an expensive event but a social event too being encouragement for those who maintained a station garden mostly in their own time and at their own expense.

It was also the end of an era, a glorious end. Diesels were replacing steam in ever increasing numbers, freight was declining, branch lines and stations were closing. Stationmasters were being replaced by station managers with larger areas of responsibility and economy was the watchword of the day. But it was great while it lasted. There was a brave new world to come, full of interest and excitement. It would have been an even braver new world if the government had given the railways more support."

Chapter Eight

Black as Night – Gangers' Tales

A great deal has been written about the wonderful views to be enjoyed from the trains traversing the Settle-Carlisle.

Considerably less is known of what goes on maintaining the fourteen tunnels covering a total distance of some four miles. Back in 1958 Bill Mitchell set to rectifying this, obtaining permission to join a tunnel gang prospecting five hundred feet below Blea Moor, at 2,629 yards the longest on the line. He had already heard how smoke from passing trains – especially those that were double-headed – might reduce visibility to nil.

The tunnel gang

By the 1930s members of the tunnel gang were paid an additional half a crown per week for working in Blea Moor. The railway company's generosity did not end there. Workers were provided with thigh length leggings and a white blanket coat. The latter was the cause of much merriment. Presumably the idea was that it made them easier to be seen from a locomotive in the darkness of the tunnel. Unfortunately these coats tended to get black and filthy rather quickly.

At the time of Bill's visit, steam was still king and the passage of trains frequent. Despite it being midsummer,

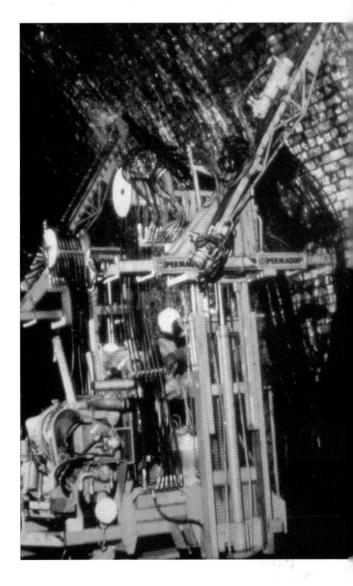

Working on the linings inside Blea Moor Tunnel, which in steam days was a near vision of Dante's inferno.

the weather outside was grey and mizzling, mist hanging about. Nothing unusual for the Settle-Carlisle. Bill's trip into a near vision of Dante's inferno was to be in the company of Mr A Gardner, chief works inspector. The tunnel gang were already present enjoying a welcome cup of tea as they waited for the day's activities to commence.

Two wagons stood on the up line, one a box type van bearing a special framework that allowed men to stand atop it while bearing a selection of hammers and spear-like objects. In the other open wagon another inspector sat holding a tough sheet of paper on which was to be recorded observations on the state of the tunnel.

Mr Gardner, by now on the roof of the van, gave a signal and seven railwaymen put their shoulders to the wheel, propelling the two wagons slowly into the tunnel. Bill walked behind this entourage in the company of Mr J E Turner, engineering assistant in the office of the District Engineer at Lancaster.

He learnt that the tunnel has a crown, haunches and sidewalls. On the sidewalls tablets periodically gave the distance from the tunnel mouth. The hammer-bearing men tapped away noting any hollow portions which were recorded. The spearmen prodded soft masonry, some of which came down. Paraffin lamps hissed as the wagons rumbled slowly forward. "Hold it," came a command followed by the sound of larger chunks of falling masonry. The position was noted for remedial work at a later date.

From far ahead came three blasts on a whistle followed by the cry, "Train on the down". Compression built in Bill's ears. The shriek of a steam whistle was heard followed by a second command. "Clear the six foot," the space between up and down lines. Folk have been injured by a wildly flapping wagon sheet on a train travelling at speed. Another shriek, this time much closer, then the train tore by, its firebox breathing a satanic glow for a few brief seconds.

Smoke billowed down from the roof of the tunnel. Fleeting impressions, the staccato drumming of wheels on rail joints, the sheer size of the train when not viewed either from afar or the safety of a platform. The smoke was not as bad as Bill had feared, nonetheless one of the gang advised him to tuck the bottoms of his trousers into his socks, "Then you won't have smoke pouring from under your collar!"

The work went on in fits and starts, incantations from the high priests up top sounding like a subterranean religious ceremony. The human-powered train passed in turn beneath the three shafts used for ventilation purposes. When built there were seven, permitting work from each to proceed in either direction from its base plus either end giving sixteen working headings. After completion four shafts were filled in. The tunnel at its greatest depth is five hundred feet below the moor, the deepest shaft being 390 feet. Each shaft is ten feet wide bearing garlands which direct the water into a downspout debouching into the tunnel drains. Blea Moor Tunnel has a summit to allow for easy drainage. Just inside its southern end it makes an abrupt change of direction. Yet so precise were the measurements that on meeting up, the various sections were only a matter of inches out requiring minimal adjustment.

There are refuges for maintenance staff to shelter, though these were not needed as the gang had possession of the up line. As they reached daylight Bill was advised by one gang member, "Wait till we get diesels, they'll be having us whitewash this tunnel." Another ventured, "Tha's bin lucky today. Tha'll nobbut need a wesh when tha gets home. Most days we need a bath – and change watter several times an' all."

A tragic accident

During the 1939-45 war Cecil Sanderson (Sandy), stationmaster at Dent, was advised of some fatalities to a gang working in the tunnel. Stopping the next train on the up, Leeds-bound line, he boarded it along with some stretchers from Home Guard stock kept in the waiting room. The accident happening around 4am it took some time for the news to reach Dent.

On board the locomotive, Sandy instructed the driver to stop at the northern end of Blea Moor Tunnel while he had a word with the ganger Charlie Campbell and a group of his men in their cabin close to the north portal. He asked for volunteers to accompany him. One man stood forward, it being later revealed that he had lost both his father and grandfather in previous accidents in this very tunnel.

They walked in front of the engine carrying paraffin lamps behind them so that the driver might see them. After a short distance there was evidence of a terrible accident smeared on the walls. The remains of the special tunnel gang based on Ribblehead looked from a distance like heaps of clothing.

The gang had entered the tunnel from the Ribblehead south end walking on the up line, facing the traffic when the sound of a train was heard from the north end approaching them. Instead of finding a recess to shelter, they stepped across onto the down line. Unbeknown to them another train carrying parcels and, being but two vans long, the fastest on the line, was bearing down on them from the opposite direction. The sound of the first drowned the second. It ploughed into the gang decimating them.

Track in the tunnel in steam days had a life expectancy of but ten years – half of that anticipated outside. That of the tunnel gang was similarly shortened. The place reeked of sulphur plus there was the prepetual drip of water.

The tunnel gang certainly earned their premium of half a crown per week.

The Long Drag

Not all trains raced through Blea Moor Tunnel. After the fourteen miles at a ruling grade of 1 in 100 from Settle Junction, many a freight train almost came to a stop on Ribblehead Viaduct if a strong westerly was blowing. The viaduct is built on a curve plus the northern end is twelve feet higher than the south. Brief respite might be gained in the cutting approaching the tunnel, yet the climb continued to midway through the tunnel to a minor summit. Many a fireman on a

A northbound goods train in the lie-by siding at Ais Gill. If a freight had struggled through Blea Moor tunnel and onto the summit, it could well be put into this siding to get up steam.

slow-moving freight would press his shovel against the tunnel wall to ensure they were still making progress – in the correct direction.

Doctor urgently required

Not far north is Hawes Junction & Garsdale as it was originally known. Now it is simply Garsdale. There was in the late 19th century no telephone connection between the junction and Hawes itself some six miles down Wensleydale. Were the doctor required two platelayers put their bogie on the line before rolling the six miles down gradient to Wensleydale's high market town. They brought it back by the simple expedient of placing it behind the brake van of the afternoon freight to the junction, then taking it in turns to hang onto the draw-bar hook.

There was not too much concern for health and safety in those days. If there was a problem, then you took whatever action was required to solve it.

In the event of serious illness the North Eastern engine would be roused from its slumbers in its own dedicated shed at Garsdale, steam raised and run down to Hawes to bring back the doctor. A second trip was made to return him. Now that is what you call personal service.

Bonniface

One explanation of the 4.25pm from Hawes bearing the name Bonniface is as follows. Mr Silcock, permanent way inspector and Mr Slater, signal and telegraph superintendent at Settle, arranged for a third-class brake carriage to run from Hellifield to Hawes Junction to carry their men. They were otherwise exposed to the severe weather their work entailed, becoming wet through and subject to prolonged illness trying to get to and from their work sites.

The service was extended to Hawes, proving to be a real boon. So much so that when the service began in 1889, one of the gangers, being so delighted to see the train coming, exclaimed, "Here's Bonniface coming" and it stuck.

Belt Pie for dinner

Around the turn of the 19th century Lemuel Cox was a tough foreman timber loader. He and his gang worked at Baron Wood between Lazonby and Armathwaite, where may still be seen the timber sidings though they are no longer connected to the Settle-Carlisle.

When the day's arduous work was over, Cox and his gang would travel to Carlisle by slow train before transferring to the up 'Scotchman' with a view to leaving the train at Skipton, a conditional stop. Actually travel on this train by the timber gang was not allowed so they had to stow their gear beneath the seats to avoid detection.

On one occasion the train had been stopped at Kirkby Stephen due to lack of steam resulting in a very slow climb to Ais Gill. In an endeavour to make up time the driver belted down the south side of the Drag from Blea Moor at well over the maximum speed of 70mph. The lateral oscillation caused by such speed in the stock of those days could be a frightening experience even to Lemuel Cox. Arriving home in a blazing temper something flipped him resulting in his taking his belt to his long-suffering wife and giving her a right hiding.

This was nothing new but this time she had had enough. When he was safely tucked up in bed she took a knife, cut up his belt and baked it in a pie. Next morning he couldn't find his belt anywhere and resorted to a piece of cord to hold up his trousers. However, when he saw the pie, he was overjoyed with its golden brown crust bragging to his mates how he would enjoy this at dinner time.

The gang used a platelayers' cabin in which to eat their meals. This housed a standard Midland stove of the type issued to signal boxes. Above the fire compartment there was a small oven on the top of which was a hotplate where inevitably lodged a kettle. Round about 12 o'clock Cox nipped into the cabin and popped his pie into the oven ready for the 12.30 break. The gang drifted in one by one with comments akin, "God, what a bloody stink", or "Somebody drying their socks or summat", and even "Smells like somebody's burning a body."

Cox eventually took his pie out of the oven, gave a contemptuous glance at his men tackling their sandwiches and hacked into the pie with his clasp knife.

Of course when the pie was opened the mystery of the appalling smell was revealed, Cox smashed it down on the floor, stamping out of the cabin amid derisive laughter and many ribald comments. "That'll larn yer Lem," plus "Ah thought she were flayed to dearth on yer" and "Wonder what she'll slice up next."

He never lived it down, though there is no record of what he said to his wife. His attitude towards her was by all accounts considerably improved.

Major pile-up avoided

On 10 May 1974 an accident occurred which might well have had disastrous consequences. A quarry lorry from one of the many quarries around Horton in Ribblesdale was taking its heavy load of one inch limestone by articulated vehicle in the direction of Settle. Approaching Langcliffe there is a tightish left hand swing onto the bridge carrying road over railway, the latter here in cutting.

The trailer swung into the parapet, demolishing twenty yards of it before falling twenty-eight feet onto the track below dragging the tractor unit with it and effectively blocking both lines. The driver, Frank Matthews, was trapped..

By chance four builders working close by rushed to the scene. Amazingly they were all members of the CRO, the cave rescue organisation based at Clapham. All rail traffic was stopped on both the up and down lines before a major pile-up occurred. The track here, apart from being in cutting is in the midst of a reverse curve restricting a driver's view to a few hundred yards.

Typical Midland Railway stove in a platelayers' cabin.
A kettle was invariably on top of the hotplate.

The CRO members realised that it would be beyond conventional means to rescue the driver so called for a mountain rescue ambulance with specialist gear. When he was eventually recovered from the steep cutting a police escort was provided to take him by ambulance to Airedale Hospital where his condition was described as 'very poorly'. He survived and I understand is still living.

It took seven hours to recover the wreckage, British Rail calling in a heavy-duty crane to recover the articulated vehicle.

Company generosity

A Hellifield ganger retired during the 1960s after forty-three years service. His railway pension was half a guinea a week. Another after retiring was called to Derby to be told he had been a good worker before being presented with £5 plus a free dinner voucher.

The accident at Langcliffe bridge on 10 May 1974, when an articulated lorry plunged through the parapet onto the tracks. All rail traffic was stopped before a major disaster occurred.

Chapter Nine

Fun Around the Fringes and On-Shed Tales

There was a certain spot in Kirkby Stephen well known to the railway fraternity from whence during the night you might look across the valley to the course of the railway illuminated by a white-hot trail of runaway wheels. In these situations – not so unusual – arrival at Kirkby Stephen East would be amidst a shower of sparks, no brake blocks and even the hangers burnt out!

During the early 1990s I chanced to meet Alec Davis who was at the time running a cafe in Kirkby Stephen. At a later date I returned with a tape machine to record his memories as a past fireman on the other railway which ran through Kirkby Stephen, the North Eastern line from Durham and Barnard Castle to Tebay and Penrith on what we now know as the West Coast main line. The station at Kirkby Stephen East was a large one, far larger than that on the Midland at Kirkby Stephen West and much more convenient for the town centre.

This area was mentioned in a previous chapter when the North Eastern line had been truncated at Hartley Quarry which Stan Hall visited on one of the last trains. The North Eastern also had a station in Appleby only some hundred yards from the Settle-Carlisle. The track from there to Kirkby Stephen is still in situ as far as Warcop where a preservation society exists. There was and indeed still is a physical connection between the two branching off to the north of Appleby (Midland) station. This provided a useful diversionary route to Carlisle via Clifton Junction and Penrith.

Fun in the jungle

I remember not so long ago when it used to be a regular event to reverse steam-hauled charter trains back up this link to let a service train pass before taking water from the water crane at the end of the up platform. The trackwork has now been improved, then it was like a jungle. Derek Soames and I, stewards on the train were in the rear coach of a twelve-coach charter being propelled into and passing through this jungle, the undergrowth at the far end being around six feet high. I remarked to Derek, "I do hope there is still some track under this lot." There was.

Stainmore

Back up the climb to Stainmore it was a formidable ruling gradient of 1 in 59 to the summit, which at 1,370 feet was some 200 feet higher than Ais Gill. In winter it was according to Alec a regular thing to hand-sand the rails when for whatever reason the locomotive sanders failed.

In the reverse direction on a loose-coupled freight you stopped at Stainmore Summit where the guard pinned down a quarter of wagon brakes. You needed a little steam to get rolling, after which the tender brake was screwed hard down and the engine steam brake applied. Having done all that was possible – you prayed. Sometimes your prayers went unanswered with the results already described. One road was designated in Kirkby yard for runaways. Common practice was for the west box signalman to route such a train onto the single track for Tebay which had a rising grade. Fine, provided there was not something already heading towards you!

Two films were made on this line over Stainmore by British Transport Films in 1955. Alec, based at Kirkby Stephen shed, was the fireman on the first one in summer. The second and more memorable, 'Snow Drift at Bleath Gill', has become a classic involving the rescue of a stranded train near Stainmore Summit. Alec received 2s 6d – plus a bar of chocolate – as a film extra.

The Tebay branch from Kirkby Stephen actually passed beneath the easternmost arch of Smardale viaduct on the Settle-Carlisle being at 130 feet the highest on the line. If you look carefully to the left when crossing this you will just glimpse the Smardale Gill Viaduct which carried this long defunct line. British Rail wanted to demolish the viaduct but being listed this was not possible. Ultimately contractors made it good, in the process gaining valuable knowledge not wasted when it came to tackling Ribblehead Viaduct.

High jinks in Smardale

For several years I was the Trust Administrator for Cumbria Wildlife Trust whose spectacular Smardale reserve follows the former trackbed for some four miles down the grade to Newbiggin on Lune, thence to Tebay. This latter section is now the realigned course of the A685. When the reserve was upgraded to a National Nature Reserve we had a grand opening ceremony with many dignitaries at the viaduct, where it was decided we would make the most of the historical aspect. It was arranged that at a signal from the Trust Director I should emerge from the Smardale direction dressed in Victorian attire including top hat. I was portraying Sir Richard Tufton, a director of the South Durham & Lancashire Union Railway, the precursor of what became a part of the North Eastern Railway.

Marching down the trackbed swinging my cane I demanded to know what all these people were doing on the line as the 12.15pm ex-Tebay was due at any moment. At this point a colleague switched on a tape recording of a similar train toiling up the grade. This was hidden in his van camouflaged in the undergrowth and operated through its battery via speakers up in the trees. You should have seen folk leap out of the way – it was so realistic!

Two points of interest. The course of this railway was surveyed by Sir Thomas Bouch, sadly better known for the ill-fated Tay Bridge which he designed. The second is that our old friend Stanley Hall was in his younger days a stationmaster on this line over Stainmore at Winton on the eastern side.

Time now to move to the southern end of the Settle-Carlisle.

Rabbity Dick

The branch from Settle Junction to Carnforth spawned several further branches, one being at Clapham. It was here one day that the legendary Richard Fawcett, otherwise known as Rabbity Dick, signalman and poacher, needing to be rid of some goats dropped them from the footbridge into an open wagon forming part of a train stopped at the signals. There is no record of their final destination.

On Shed – Skipton with Mickey Venn

Down at Skipton, Mickey Venn was on a stationary locomotive when it was struck by a bolt of lightning. He recalls a strong smell of sulphur but no ill effects.

"I was firing a little shunting engine at Skipton which wasn't pulling too well. One trick you could use was to fit an item known as a 'jimmy' across the blast pipe in the smokebox. This improved the blast no end. That tanker went and sounded like a Ferrari.

Still in Skipton there had been an audacious theft from a sealed van load of spirits – whisky – carried in barrels inside. The thieves had drilled a hole right through the base of the van and into one of the barrels. My driver and I later heard two CID men discussing how they were going to catch the culprits next time. They would be inside the van waiting for them.

We had both had trouble with the police nicking us for having defective lights and this was pay-back time. Next time a van load of spirits arrived we were on duty that night. We shunted that van all round Skipton yard finishing with an over-exuberant shove into a set of buffers. They never did catch the culprits.

The storeman at Skipton was about to retire, looking forward to his gold watch. He approached me as he was in big trouble. Among other things he had charge of a large oil tank filled with A1 locomotive oil which just happened to be ideal for use on cars and motorbikes. Its level was unacceptably low. I went to bed thinking about it.

In the morning I had the solution. A pile of surplus bricks dropped in the tank was the answer, raising the level to an acceptable height and ensuring the storeman received his gold watch."

Embsay Junction

From Skipton the main line heads down the Aire Valley for Leeds and Bradford. There still exists the truncated line to Grassington veering off in Skipton station. A mile out of town this split again to form the Ilkley and Otley branch, a useful diversionary route in case the main line was blocked. As far as Bolton Abbey this line has been preserved as the Yorkshire Dales Railway.

George Horner spent some time as relief signalman at boxes in this area being on duty at Embsay Junction when a mishap on the main Aire Valley line caused all traffic to be routed via

Embsay, Bolton Abbey and Ilkley. This entailed sidetracking several freight trains up the Grassington branch to allow faster traffic the road. The various crews retreated to a brakevan doubtless for a brew and possibly a hand of cards being aware they were likely to be there for some time.

George was just enjoying a well-earned pipe when he was conscious of a fireman sprinting past his box heading for a nearby wood.

Called out George, "Ist'a going for relief lad?"

"No, I'm going into this wood for some sticks, mi blooming fire's gone out."

What a stink!

Derek Soames remembers Embsay as being quieter than many stations where he had worked. There was a local tannery in the village for which cow hides would arrive by rail in an open wagon. He had nothing to do with these but imagine in summer the fresh cow hides covered with bluebottles and maggots and next thing infested by crows feasting on them!

Royal Train notices. Derek Soames did a stint as porter at Bolton Abbey, which was regularly visited by King George V during the shooting season.

A runaway!

On another occasion George was off-duty in the area of Bolton Abbey box, another at which he was a relief signalman. He popped in to have a word with his mate. The down pick-up goods was on its return from Guiseley to Skipton. The locomotive propelled its train into a running loop on the up side. The procedure here was for the shunter to uncouple the brakevan which was then fly-shunted into a stub end, the guard running alongside to clamber aboard and apply the brake.

On this occasion for whatever reason the guard missed getting on board. The signalman saw what was happening and to avoid an expensive pile-up at the buffers, opened the points at the other end. The brakevan entered the main line, passed under the bridge and out of sight.

Enquired George of his mate, "Where's he going to land up then?"

"Oh, don't worry, he'll be back."

Not for nothing was the stretch from Bolton Abbey to Addingham known as going over the Alps.

So they lit their pipes and waited and in due course the brakevan rolled slowly back into sight, took the points into the loop and the guard didn't miss it this time.

Make way for the King

Derek Soames remembers a stint as porter at Bolton Abbey, a quietish sort of place, though the Deveonshire Arms Hotel had a regular supply of fish arriving by train. It was his job to deliver it – pronto.

More importantly King George V had his own private siding where the royal train would be berthed when he came north during the shooting season. It was known as the Kings Siding, in Derek's time there still being a pair of steps to hand used by His Majesty to access his saloon.

Wensleydale

The name Sidney Weighell is synonymous with railways. Long before he became General Secretary of the National Union of Railwaymen, he worked his way up from cleaner to fireman then driver. A memory he held dear was frying up on the shovel when waiting for the road.

The Weighell family were steeped in railways, four members clocking up an amazing 176 years service between them, much of this being on the Northallerton to Garsdale branch, the Hawes-Garsdale section being Contract Number Five on the Midland Railway extension to Carlisle.

Sidney recounts how on one trip to Garsdale he had a slip of a lad acting as fireman. They were well under way travelling against the grade when he casually enquired of him if he had remembered to top up the tanks either side of the engine. He hadn't! Panic, the train was going nowhere without full tanks so some quick thinking was needed. At a passing place on the single

LNER 2-4-2 tank about to leave Garsdale for Northallerton. One of the regular drivers was Sidney Weighell, who later became General Secretary of the National Union of Railwaymen.

Railwaymen gather on Garsdale station platform prior to departure of the branch train to Northallerton. There is no sign of any passengers – a not unusual occurrence!

Hellifield shed continued to thrive into the 1960s.

Above: A busy scene in August 1961 with several locomotives in steam.

Below: Standard Class 4 76083 at the coaling stage.

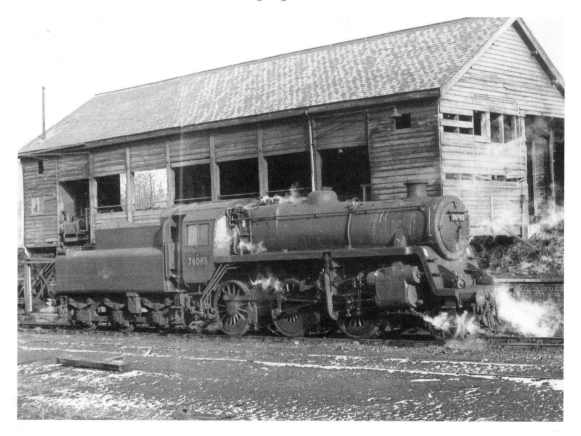

line threading the valley, they met another train going down the grade back to Northallerton. Don't ask how but Sid persuaded the driver to swap engines with him, this accomplished after a deal of shunting. This practice was quite out of order. Questions were later asked by inspectors, though it seems the truth never did leak out.

By the way , the various railway members were identified by pseudonym, Sid being known as 'Bogie Weighell'.

The Lancashire & Yorkshire road

On the road (track) from Hellifield to Blackburn there are some formidable gradients. Proceeding southwards a freight from Carlisle to Manchester was struggling and popped (whistled) for a banker at Clitheroe. This would assist from Whalley. It rapidly became clear that the help being provided was minimal. Entering Whalley tunnel the fireman had had enough. With the permission of his driver, he relieved himself on the shovel which was promptly shoved in the fire. The resulting stink ensured they quickly received a mighty shove!

Not that many years ago Bill and I were on board a steam charter returning from Carlisle to Preston. The locomotive was struggling having twice stopped to clear the fire and raise steam. No reflection on the enginemen, simply rotten coal.

We disembarked at Hellifield hours late. Here the fireman again made strenuous efforts to raise steam. He was unsuccessful, the train later stalling on Wilpshire bank where help had to be sought from a diesel. Two elderly ladies annouced their intention to climb down and walk home. They had to be restrained. Eventually landfall was made at 2am in Preston where a sort of Dunkirk spirit prevailed, folk giving others lifts as close as possible to their homes. Some had to be put up in hotels on sofas, there being a major event in town.

Hellifield shed

Some more tales from Mickey Venn, the first over the boss at Hellifield who had as penance put him on cleaning a massive filthy rusty austerity locomotive. He was distraught, it was going to take hours. Driver Jack Dugdale, by now confined to shed and shunting duties due to defective eyesight, came to his rescue.

"Go to the store and get some graphite oil to mix with mineral oil." Mickey did this and within about four hours this old tub was positively gleaming. Just long enough for him to be allowed off shift. Within hours the loco would be back to normal as the cold air negated the effect of its massage.

"Once my colleagues locked me in a locomotive smokebox after I had given them too much lip and they threatened to light a fire.

Another day my driver Jack Dugdale was shunting a loco onto the wheel drop. Suddenly from the smoke trough above a baby little owl dropped out in a bit of a state. It was befriended by several crews and, mice being plentiful, did not go short of food. Eventually it recovered and was released back into the wild by Jack.

Ted Preston, the foreman at Hellifield, had a worse bark than bite. One day I was knocked up when there was no work for me. I might have claimed a day's pay but did not. Ted did not forget. At that time I was a seventeen year old cleaner. He moved me up to labouring for three hours then a first turn at firing. Magic. That week I took home £26 giving mum a large slice which pleased her no end, times being tough."

Driver Teddy Earnshaw went to collect his pay from the wages clerk at Hellifield just before 5pm and was told to come back the next day. Now Teddy was a thrifty sort of chap, a non-drinker and had a few bob put away. He didn't go back next day nor indeed next week. In fact his wages mounted up for six months before authority, getting worried at the amount of cash they were holding, pleaded with him to collect his money. He never had trouble with that clerk again.

Rowland Earnshaw, Teddy's brother, was in charge of maintaining the ashpit and tubs for coaling at Hellifield. He was fastidious over his moustache, which was waxed into two points not unlike Agatha Christie's Poirot.

He had his job off to a T. So much so that he could do it in six hours and would slope off early. He was suspended twice but had to be invited back as nobody else could match his work rate!

Finally Mickey recounts how a diesel ran away heading north and crashed into the rear of another train near Helwith Bridge. This necessitated a large call-out of recovery specialists. "I had the job of contacting them pronto. I was always getting into scrapes, as a result managing to accumulate not one but three number one forms. I was in big trouble. After the panic my boss called me in.

'Come in and sit down, you did a great job raising that crew, if I can help you just let me know.'

'Funny you should say that, will you scrub those number one forms?'

He did, bless him."

Chapter Ten

Return of Steam –
and the Ugly Threat of Closure

George Durrant Hinchcliffe is a remarkable man. Initially he trained as an engineer. This was followed by service in the Royal Navy during the war where at one time he was the youngest Chief Petty Officer in the Senior Service. Next he had a switch of career to teaching, becoming a deputy school headmaster.

George Hinchcliffe, photographed at Carnforth station during 2008.

All this he forsook to accept the chance of a lifetime as engineering manager with the first of two tours undertaken by 'Flying Scotsman' to the USA in 1969. After the recovery of the locomotive to these shores, he took up the post of managing director at Steamtown, Carnforth, the last remaining steam shed number 10A. This is where I first met him back in 1979.

1976 was the centenary of completion of the Settle-Carlisle Railway. Sadly steam in the form of 4472 'Flying Scotsman' was only allowed as far north as Settle station, where there were a great many festivities taking place. In passing it is worth noting that Bill Mitchell, a life-long champion of the line, put on a slide show one evening around this time about the railway. This nearly did not take place, it only being realised at the eleventh hour that the venue, the station booking hall, relied solely on gas. A local electrician at short notice strung a mammoth extension to the stationmaster's house.

The initial idea of putting steam back on the Settle-Carlisle was down to David Ward, then Special Services Manager at Euston. His request had been turned down on several occasions due to apparent problems with the overhead wires at Carlisle. Steam was allowed to go under the wires at Carnforth and George could not see the problem at Carlisle.

As he recalls: "I repeatedly talked to David about this, pointing out that there was no need to go under the wires. I had got a way of doing it having looked at the track layout there. David said that if he set up a meeting with Mike Carrier at Carlisle would I go there, talk to him and see what might be done?

I replied in the affirmative. This is before the ugly head of 'Let's shut the Settle-Carlisle line' got under way. I met up with Mike Carrier, who was Assistant Area Manager Carlisle, a nice

The glorious return of steam – 1. Black Five 5407 struggling to make 10mph at Blea Moor on icy rails on a wild day.

person and extremely capable, running a very very good station. He had got together the two representatives of the unions, the NUR and ASLEF. As you might guess, we went to a pub where we discussed the difficulty.

What I proposed was that the steam engine should work over the S&C, possibly from Skipton, another engine having already taken the train over the first leg from Carnforth as there were no turning facilities at either Skipton or Hellifield. The steam would be taken off at London Road Junction some quarter of a mile outside Citadel station, Carlisle, being replaced with a diesel after the steam locomotive had negotiated the tight curve into Upperby shed area where it would be serviced. The diesel of course hauled the train around the cord line into the station.

After some time for the passengers to enjoy Carlisle an electric locomotive would take the train back to Carnforth via Shap. The following week the procedure would be reversed. The locomotive already at Carlisle would take over from the electric-hauled leg over Shap running the train back to Skipton where a second steam engine having travelled light engine from Carnforth would complete the third leg back there.

Well I put this to Mike Carrier and the two union men who immediately agreed. It is true to say that we had been drinking beer, I being in the position of needing some relief as did the union officials. Sadly I cannot remember their names. As we stood side by side one of them said to his friend, 'We don't mind taking a steam engine into Carlisle do we?'

His colleague replied, 'No, we don't mind, we know what we are doing, we will have a steam engine into Carlisle, save a deal of bother.'

So that is the way it was set up. David Ward was more than happy opining that it would be nice for the first train over the Drag to be in honour of Bill Harvey, retired Locomotive Shed Master at Norwich. He was instrumental in overseeing the restoration of 'Green Arrow', which hauled that first train, the Norfolkman, on 25 March 1978. He accompanied the locomotive as engineer in charge during its early years of preserved operation. It seems a V2 had never before been over the Long Drag. Everything went according to plan. Either 'Flying Scotsman' or a Black Five took the outward leg, Carnforth to Skipton.

The trains were put into service during that first season in 1978 being known as the Cumbrian Mountain Express, the late Bernard Staite having a deal to do with their operation.

Many people have claimed to have been instrumental in the return of steam over the S&C. This however is a true story, the moral behind it being that if negotiating with union officials, these matters should initially be handled in a pub, final decisions being made in a public convenience!"

....

"The Settle-Carlisle Line had been under threat for a very long time. It lost most of its freight traffic plus the passenger traffic dwindled alarmingly. We had always been aware of this, though with the steam trains going along the line it helped enormously, not just to get traffic over it but getting people to ride it to enjoy the wonders of scenery through which it passes. It is perhaps the most scenic route in the whole of Britain, certainly in England.

While this threat hung over the line there were celebrations going on to mark the 150th anniversary of the Liverpool to Manchester Railway during 1979. I was at the time chairman of SLOA, the Steam Locomotive Operators' Association, and responsible on their behalf and British Rail to get all the steamable locomotives to the colliery site near Shildon.

A dinner was arranged at the National Railway Museum to celebrate the events of the 150th anniversary. I was invited as chairman of SLOA along with a considerable number of important guests, including William Whitelaw MP, the Duke of Wellington and Sir Peter Parker, the chairman of British Rail.

The latter I knew well having met him several times through Bill McAlpine, and we were on christian name terms. After we had finished dinner, as usual it was necessary to visit the convenience where I found myself between Sir Peter Parker, left; William Whitelaw, right; with right of him the Duke of Wellington. I could not resist remarking that I had never before relieved myself in such illustrious company in my life. They all laughed and we had an excellent evening.

A few months later I was travelling to London on one of the morning trains from Lancaster to meet David Ward. Who should be sitting in the train not far from me but William Whitelaw MP with a bodyguard, he being Northern Ireland Secretary at the time. As I went to the buffet car he looked up saying, 'I know you, we stood together didn't we?' I answered in the affirmative and had a chat with him. That was that.

The proposed closure of the Settle-Carlisle line rears its ugly head and I get involved with a committee consisting of local authorities, the Cumbria Tourist Board and many other organisations anxious to save the line. I went to innumerable meetings, there being a time when it seemed that the government appeared to be in a position to accept that it had to be closed or to close it.

I still travelled on the morning train from Lancaster to London and on another occasion met William Whitelaw again. He invited me to join him and we discussed the closure proposal with which he was fully aware. He knew of running steam over the line, it being close to his constituency. He told me that he had made some suggestions and 'I think you will find one of the ministers is going to have a look at it. Would it help if I suggested that it would be a good thing if he talked to you?'

I said that it certainly would. In fact it didn't happen. My recollection is that Paul Channon went to view it along with Michael Portillo.

A week or two later I was again on the London train and once more met William Whitelaw. I enquired as to news of the Settle-Carlisle line and he replied that he thought it would be good news.

It was the best news."

Return of steam – 2.
Sheriff Brow Number One viaduct being
crossed by the unique Class 8 'Duke of
Gloucester'.

Return of steam – 3.
Midland Compound 1000 and Jubilee 5690 'Leander' head the
Cumbrian Mountain Pullman near Armathwaite, February 1983.

*Return of steam – 4.
'Duchess of Sutherland' enters Mallerstang
north of Birkett Tunnel.*

Chapter Eleven

Renovations and Refurbishment

During the winter of 1984/85 the line over Ribblehead viaduct was singled at the behest of Alan King, then Assistant Chief Civil Engineer London Midland Region. Explaining his reasoning to me Alan opined tongue in cheek that this course spread the load throughout the width of the viaduct and that a train might be passing over it when both parapets fell away simultaneously, yet leaving the passengers perfectly safe – disconcerted possibly – yet perfectly safe.

Alan was in fact fighting a rearguard action, trying to save the line from closure. He reckoned that singling the line would gain two years' breathing space during which time hopefully a solution would be found to the problems of Ribblehead.

A replacement for Ribblehead Viaduct

During the late seventies British Rail had evolved a series of intriguing options to replace this viaduct – various types of bridge, even an embankment. Eventually a trial repair gave an accurate assessment of the cost for full renovation. The rest is history. Sadly, Alan died at the early age of sixty-one. At least he had the satisfaction of seeing Ribblehead fully restored. I think of Alan as the man who did not close the Settle-Carlisle. An oblique compliment but none the less sincere. Don't forget he was ultimately responsible for the safety of passengers and staff passing over it.

A day to remember

One day I shall never forget and it was down to him. I had expressed a wish to travel in the cab of a DMU (diesel multiple unit) from Settle to Carlisle first thing in the morning – the 'Early Bird', which then left Skipton at 06.15 on weekdays. He fixed it for me, though it involved travelling to Carnforth to meet and return with a traction inspector, Paul Jameson, to Skipton.

Paul lived at Fulwood in Preston, cycling into the town centre at 2.30am to catch the down Barrow parcels. I met the train at Carnforth, a class 31 with just one van. Paul was perhaps understandably less enthusiastic than I as we drove across country to Skipton. When he found that I wanted to create a photographic slide record to use in an audio-visual show on the S&C he mellowed considerably. After mugs of tea in the mess room at Skipton he became positively loquacious.

The DMU screen had been thoroughly cleaned before we set off. It was one of those balmy September mornings with an autumn mist rising from the fields and lineside as we passed Settle Junction before attacking the ruling 1 in 100 grade to Ribblehead. The diesel multiple units were

*Alan King, Assistant Chief Civil Engineer,
photographed beside a snowplough at Ais Gill.*

*Ribblehead – both parapets might
fall away simultaneously!*

Tony Freschini, resident engineer on the Ribblehead project. He is seen here on the other side of Whernside at the south end of Dent Head viaduct, itself under renovation.

Winter sunshine highlights Ribblehead viaduct at the time it was under repair. The massive structure is dwarfed by the surrounding landscape.

Clearing the ballast before repairs started on the viaduct. Weather conditions are 'normal' with the summit of Whernside shrouded in low cloud.

The Ribblehead scaffolders, who were a tough crowd of 'hard hat' men.

Opposite: Ribblehead viaduct is no stranger to scaffolding, as seen here in the early 1960s when much brickwork under the arches was replaced. The figures at bottom right indicate the massive scale of the structure.

not the fastest thing on eight wheels but they were comfortable with a rolling gait which might induce sleep.

But not today. Approaching Garsdale the down distant semaphore was off against the rising sun. That mist was still swirling around as we swayed down Mallerstang only clearing beyond Appleby.

Arriving at Carlisle, Paul enquired as to my plans for return. Service train I replied.

Why not, he suggested, go back with him again in the cab. No second bidding was required. Just a quick dash into town to visit Jessops for more film. A magical day!

Ribblehead Viaduct repairs

Tony Freschini was the resident engineer on the Ribblehead project, Geoff Bounds the project manager. Both became friends and indeed still are. I interviewed Tony in one of the portakabins which formed in effect a modern-day shanty town.

His memories include, as if one might forget it, the weather. It did its damnedest with frequent heavy rain. This was just something that the

The awesome spectacle of twenty-four hour working. At night in this wild landscape it seemed an unbelievable sight.

operatives had to put up with. The major problem was the wind. On the bridge – which is the way the contractors referred to the viaduct – it was decided that a safe wind speed when working from scaffolding was 50 mph. At deck level they simply had to put up with it, though there was a fair degree of shelter behind the parapet which tended to deflect the wind above those working there.

George Horner used to tell the tale of a ganger walking over the viaduct, having his peaked cap blown off and flying under the nearest arch before landing back on his head, albeit back to front. I reckon this was one tale on which he pushed his luck just that bit too far.

The scaffolders were a tough crowd. Everything they touched involved scaffolding, even a washing line and a bed, one of the latter of which they were short. The mattress was it seems formed of planks lifted wet off the moor. One had in a former life been a taxidermist, another a butcher, so they were forever catching rabbits, skinning them and hanging them on a line until required.

Obviously some strange things occurred during the renovation, none more so than one cold January morning when one of the contractors knocked at the door of Tony's cabin with the news that there was a coffin on the bridge. Tony's reaction was somewhat like that of Stan Hall as already recounted, "Was it the first of April?"

Reassured that it wasn't and finally convinced that this was for real, he climbed the 100 odd feet to deck level and there a near quarter of a mile away was something propped up in a refuge. As he got nearer it became apparent that there was indeed a coffin stood on end. More than that it bore a plaque with one word, 'Walter'. The lid was laid loosely against it and an arm was hanging out.

Tony and the three men accompanying him approached. He was not convinced that what he was seeing was for real so tore back the lid, emitting a scream. His three colleagues fled in terror – and the coffin was empty – bar a rubber arm.

As I suggested to him, it was indeed 'armless!

Dent Head

Other viaducts received remedial treatment at a later date. One such was Dent Head. I had permission to visit this and remember in particular one evening when I had arranged to meet Ian Ibbotson, the clerk of works, in the lull between two shifts around 9pm on an unusually still November night.

He was alone and had seen a ghost. Certainly his hair was stood on end. The ghost transpired to be formed by smoke rising genie like in the still air from the perpetual fire through a willow bush. They have a lot to answer for those willow bushes.

Another day I arrived to find an obvious atmosphere at Dent Head. The contractor, Construction Group North, had given notice the day before that come the end of the contract the workforce at Dent Head would all be made redundant. There was simply no more money in the kitty.

These skilled men worked in all weathers in all seasons in remote locations. Some of them had twenty or thirty years' service, others had followed their fathers before. One of them told me how they had heard the news.

The coffin on the viaduct!

"We walked off the job on Wednesday afternoon at 2.30pm. At 2.45 we had a phone call to say it would be wound up by 31st March. All the lads are agreed that although they are redundant they are still going to finish this job on time. Shows they have got guts doesn't it?"

Politicians and overpaid captains of industry may care to dwell on this. I well remember that on the concrete haunch designed to carry the still-to-be-installed waterproof membrane someone had spray painted, "You won't make foreman now Stirrup."

Happily several of them formed a new company, Right Track Construction, which installed the waiting room on the newly created northbound platform at Ribblehead. For many, many years there had only been a platform on the up line, causing George Horner to remark that it was the place from which "one always departed, nivver arrived". I was present when it was officially opened. The weather, it was foul!

Crown Street Bridge

At the northern end of the line in Carlisle there is a bottleneck, Crown Street Bridge. By 1993 the bridge was life-expired. Tony Freschini was given the job of replacing it.

This involved removing all lines south of Carlisle station plus even a slice off some of the platforms. Clockwise these served the routes to Newcastle, Leeds, Lancaster and the south, and the Cumberland coast.

Clearly there was a deal of preparatory work. Tony and his team were allowed just fifty-six hours over a weekend for removal of the old and installation of the new bridge. In fact there were two new structures to replace the former wrought-iron bridges.

An amazing piece of mechanical engineering in the form of a bridge transporter carried on 128 wheels, each of which was capable of swinging independently through 360 degrees, was employed to move these massive items which weighted several hundred tons apiece.

The finely synchronised movements of the bridge transporter system and all of the jacking requirements were managed by a single operator. He directed the movements using a portable

Looking north over Dent Head viaduct – note the walkway.

Left: Ian Ibbotson (right), clerk of works at Dent Head viaduct. This was not the occasion that he had seen a ghost! Right: Preparing the concrete haunch for the waterproof membrane at Dent Head.

Tight fit! A 128-wheel transporter inches the new bridge into position at Crown Street, Carlisle. Tony Freschini and his team had just 56 hours to complete the operation during a tense weekend in 1993.

Earlier repairs at Dent Head viaduct in the 1960s. A goods train is heading south behind an 8F 2-8-0.

Contrasts at Hellifield in the 1960s. Above: On a summer afternoon in 1960s there are few signs of change as Crab 42883 storms through the up platform with a Carlisle - Stourton freight. The signal box at the north end is still active, as are the engine sheds on the right.

Chaos and mass trespass on the tracks on August 11th, 1968, as 70013 'Oliver Cromwell' calls with the so-called 'Last Steam Train on British Railways'.

manual control.

The first section of the old bridge was removed and trundled along Crown Street to a site which once accommodated the former goods avoiding lines. Here stood two new sections of steel bridge on a massive scaffold framework. A second such framework was prepared to accept the old bridge sections.

Problems started as the old wrought-iron bridge proved to be considerably heavier than the new, as a result of which the scaffolding began to buckle and sink. Tony recounts how with permission they had to break into a builder's yard (it being a weekend) to scavenge more supports. In retrospect he recalls the site name, Bog Junction, which he reckons should have put him on guard.

That apart the new bridge went in on time, the only other unforeseen problem concerned a local who claimed his airspace had been infringed by the transporter lifting its load above his premises and demanding compensation. Tony's reply may not be printed here.

Hellifield Station refurbishment

During 1994 it was the turn of Hellifield station to receive refurbishment. This fine Midland Railway station built during the Victorian era was by then unstaffed, being, to put it mildly, in 'one helluva state'. Again, I was fortunate in obtaining permission to record the demolition and refurbishment.

Peter Ainsworth was clerk of works, while project manager Geoff Bounds allowed me to record his views on the enterprise.

"In January of this year [1994] we commenced the works. It's not been without its share of low points. Around March/April we had a building completely wrecked, no roof on, walls falling in, no floors or windows. We really began to wonder just what we had set ourselves to.

April 16th we put on the new roof trusses. That was the turning point. From thereon in it was putting a building back together again. Although it has taken another four or five months to do that and achieve completion, the end result is very rewarding, particularly the standard of renovation which is a credit to everyone involved. I could not have wished for a finer swansong to my time on the Settle-Carlisle Railway."

Peter was, indeed probably still is, a mountain of a man. He took me inside one of the ground floor rooms to describe the state of the structure. The façade he found well built and sound, yet inside there were bits of timber here and bits there with bricks on end as fillers to support the interior walls. Indeed if you leant against one you would probably go right through. Which is exactly what happened.

On another wild January day, Peter from his portakabin when glancing out noticed one of the tall chimney stacks apparently move in the gale. Closer examination proved that it was indeed waving about in the wind. Repairs to the stack were accomplished as soon as the gale abated.

Above Left: Hellifield station prior to the commencement of renovation in January 1994. The once proud structure was by then little more than an unstaffed shell.

Above right: Peter Ainsworth, clerk of works for Hellifield station renovation, inspects a swaying chimneystack at rooftop height.

Right: The turning point came when new roof trusses were fitted in mid-April 1994 and it was then possible to start putting the building back together. Here the present café area is being fitted out.

As at Ribblehead viaduct, twenty-four hour working was introduced in order to complete the renovation as soon as possible.

152

The finished station looking down from the hillside beyond. It provides an amazing contrast with the pre-January 1994 view.

Repainted Midland insignia and Wyverns.

The finished station is officially opened by W R (Bill) Mitchell in late 1994. Holding the sign is project manager Geoff Bounds and with him is Val Hughes, who headed up Railtrack's property team at York.

Incidentally there is or rather was a wonderful view south over the junction from this point. This was only available while the station was roofless.

An interesting item in one of the downstairs rooms was a cast iron bath, possibly for the benefit of the stationmaster when he got into a lather over some of the antics of his porters, years even decades before.

Geoff Bounds concludes with this:

"I think potentially that the Settle-Carlisle has got a big future. Paradoxically the privatisation of the railways, the way in which they have been privatised, gives the opportunity for other train operators to come on board and use the line as it has plenty of spare capacity. This allows the line to be paid fairly for the trains that use it. We had a previous situation of diversionary services and charter specials that really were not paying their way. They were using it and getting all the benefits of this fabulous railway. All that has now been changed."

Twenty-four hour working was the rule during the refurbishment. One night, Bill Mitchell, Bob Anderson the official photographer and myself had permission to scale the banking near the site of the one-time locomotive shed to obtain photographs of the floodlit station. The covering of birch which now invades the site had yet to take hold. It was just on midnight when Bob placed one foot in a rabbit hole, gave a strangled cry and went bowling down the bank. When we reached him, he was nursing a sprained ankle yet still clutching his beloved Hasselblad camera to his chest.

The greater part of the station is leased to West Coast Railways, many charter trains starting their journeys here or stopping to take on water. A group of enthusiasts have taken on maintenance of some of the ground floor buildings. The cafe has reopened on a daily basis and regular events are held, not all with a railway theme. A 'Brief Encounter' is resurrected when specials stop at the station, though the penny-ha'penny cup of tea is definitely a thing of the past.

Looking to the future, the Blackburn line is seeing increased traffic not least from the regular Manchester to Clitheroe service. How long before this is extended into Hellifield and the south bay reinstated to accommodate it?

Hellifield South Junction. The signalman looks out of his box to watch 858 'Lord Nelson' on its way to an exhibition at Liverpool Road station, Manchester, in August 1980.

Peter Akrigg, the last lampman on the Settle-Carlisle line, at work on signals at Hellifield.

Last light at Ribblehead.

Conclusion

Sometime, someone, somewhere, remarked: "The Settle-Carlisle Railway, the King Lear of Railroads, an epic route conceived in a fit of rage and driven recklessly across the kind of terrain the SAS might choose for endurance training."

Sentiments doubtless echoed by many thousands of railway navvies. SAS recruits have yet to sample its sometime waterbound, snow-covered, gale-wracked midwinter joys.

That said, possibly the fit of rage referred to was appropriate to the Midland Railway Board who, when having at the eleventh hour reached an agreement to use the rails of the London & North Western Railway via Ingleton and Low Gill to reach Carlisle, were thwarted by Parliament who refused them an abandonment order.

One thing they did not do was to drive a line recklessly over the high Pennines. Their route went through mountains and over remote valleys, always aiming at being a serious competitor to the East and West Coast railways in their 'Race to the North.' The Settle-Carlisle when opened in 1875 was designed for seventy miles per hour running!

A recent survey carried out in the USA by NBC News listed the S&C among its Top Ten 'Greatest Railway Journeys in the World'. It eclipsed the Trans Siberian Railway and the course of the Orient Express, only being pipped by the Blue Train in South Africa. Only second, oh dear!

Bishop Eric Treacy, the Railway Bishop and a man I greatly admire – though sadly never met – once remarked that the three wonders of the northern world were York Minster, Hadrian's Wall and the Settle-Carlisle Railway. Not necessarily in that order. In one of my AV shows on the railway I promoted him unwittingly not once but twice to Archbishop. He remains thus. He deserved it.

Our old friends Geoff Bounds, Tony Freschini, Stan Hall and David Ward, though all now retired, still play an active role in assisting the Friends of the Settle Carlisle and its associated companies to promote the line. They have been joined by Ron Cotton, now a vice-president of FoSCL. Ron was appointed by British Rail back in the eighties to oversee 'smooth closure'. He did a remarkable job marketing this unique railway to the n'th degree, requiring trains to be extended and duplicated to cater for the crowds that flocked to it. Sadly for British Rail, yet thankfully for practically everyone else, he failed miserably in his appointed task.

According to Hansard, there were two petitions to Parliament on 28 November 1988 from Eric Martlew (Carlisle) and David Curry (Skipton and Craven), the latter signed by 10,000 people. These lay upon the table until Commons Written Answers on 7 April 1989 when Paul Channon, then Secretary of State for Transport, said:

"I have now completed my consideration of British Rail's proposal to close the Settle-Carlisle Railway. Having reviewed all the evidence, I have decided to refuse closure consent for this line as well as for the associated Blackburn-Hellifield line. A number of factors have changed since I announced that I was minded to give consent to closure."

There followed a good deal more. The foregoing was however the nub of it.

It is a salutary thought that the Midland Railway company took seven long years to build the Settle-Carlisle line. British Rail took just as long in their endeavours to close it. Since then and to their credit, they and their successors have like the Midland before, rolled up their sleeves and got stuck into making this once more a railway to be proud of.

Settle-Carlisleitis is spreading and there is no known cure.

Enjoy it!

Illustrations

All illustrations not credited below are by the author or from his collection.

Line drawings and photo on page 124 (bottom) by Peter Fox.
Andrew Griffiths: Page 3
Donald Binns collection: 56
Gordon Hodgson: 68, 69, 84
Bob Slater: 117
J W Armstrong: 123 (bottom)
David Joy collection: 124 (top), 155 (top + bottom)
Gavin Morrison: 134/35
Yorkshire Post Newspapers:143
W R Mitchell: 149 (bottom)
John M Hammond: 150 (top)
British Railways: 150 (bottom)